RUN TO THE FIRE

RUN TO THE FIRE

*Leadership Lessons from the Arctic Circle to the Silicon Valley
and Back Home to a State in Crisis*

Steve Obsitnik

Published in the United States by Bancroft Hall Books.

Library of Congress Cataloging-in-Publication Data

Names: Obsitnik, Steve, author.

Title: Run to the fire: leadership lessons from the Arctic Circle to the Silicon Valley and back home to a state in crisis.

Identifiers: Hardcover.

Subjects: Family, values and influences./Education—mindsets and networks./Military, Service—leadership skills and problem-solving./Business: Innovation, tech startups, team building and relationships/Politics: Service, campaigning, steps to restoring fiscal security.

ISBN 978-0-9643209-1-8

Printed in the U.S.A. by LSC Communications

10 9 8 7 6 5 4 3 2 1

Book design: campbell + company
Cover photo: Megan Will

DEDICATION

To my parents, who gave me the values and foundations that have steered me in life.

And to Suzanne and our daughters, Kayden and Kira,
who fill each day with love, learning and laughter.

The best way to predict your future is to create it.

— *Abraham Lincoln*

TABLE OF CONTENTS

PREFACE

Steve Obsitnik in his book, *Run to the Fire,* recounts the lessons he has learned from both moments of challenge and success, and the leadership style he has forged from them. From a kid growing up in Connecticut to his time at the US Naval Academy, the submarine force and years as a CEO of several high technology companies, Steve shares his unique perspective on leadership and how we all should run towards adversity and opportunity.

Let me tell you why Steve and this book have had an impact on me. I am, first and foremost, a proud Connecticut native and resident. I have lived and worked in Connecticut for almost my entire life. I went to school here, met my wife here and I am now raising my family here. In 1980, my father, Bob Lederer, had a vision to start a manufacturing and printing company, which customized everyday items like cups, bags, pens and thousands of other products. He founded Prime Line in Stamford and later moved to Bridgeport. Growing up as a kid and young adult, I always felt that Connecticut was an innovative state with the inflow of companies and multinational corporations. It was vibrant.

I am now proud to run the company, extending my father's legacy. Throughout my time both working for and managing Prime, we have been proud to be a Connecticut company. In the early 2000s, we had designed an advanced, state-of-the-art manufacturing facility in Bridgeport. We were all in with Connecticut. The terrorist attacks on 9/11 changed our business, like many others, and we put that project on hold. It inserted tremendous uncertainty to our growth plans. With strong leadership and a determined team focused on hard work and execution, we continued to grow organically, all while striving to stay a Connecticut-based company. Today, we have built Prime to over 650 employees and we now occupy four of the five buildings in our office park while we are looking to expand.

However, since 9/11, the headwinds of doing business here have only grown stronger and stronger. Over the past several years, my sense is that any claims of a 'New Economic Reality' for Connecticut does not really allow manufacturing and other industries to thrive in the state any longer. We hear the talking points around why electricity prices are soaring, taxes keep rising and our costs around healthcare and worker's compensation march higher. The unintended consequences have hurt many of the people that these policies have tried to help. This 'New Economic Reality' has an unfortunate reality for my employees specifically a higher cost of living, falling housing prices, and wavering school systems. At the same time, many other states and their leaders have been actively recruiting our business to what they deem as a brighter horizon. This outreach happens on a regular basis. As any responsible owner or fiduciary would, we have undertaken studies to see what effect moving our manufacturing location to other states would have on our operations. The results are stunning. One example is that utilities savings alone are almost half of our current cost here. Though these other locations offer a financial windfall, we have remained in our state because we are dedicated to our home and to our employees' stability and livelihoods. And let's be clear, the quality of our work force we have here in Connecticut is better than the other states that have reached out to us. That being said, other regions of the country are improving their trained workers. However, the Connecticut that I am passionate about, that I raised my family in and I am proud to be in, is changing, and not for the better. Yet it is not too late for our great state!

While I have been wrestling with Prime's future, I confided in my good friend, Steve Obsitnik, my frustrations in the process of interacting with our state leadership. I have known Steve for more than ten years, and he is one of the smartest, most generous people I have ever met. He is level-headed and clear-minded. As I explained the challenges I faced, Steve was visibly concerned and helped me think through the various options for our business. He too grew up in Connecticut, and he too came to realize that our state had drifted away from the economic hub that we remembered it to be. I joined his cause, Imagine Connecticut, which brought people together to brainstorm how we can become a top 10 job creation state yet again. His leadership galvanized over 15,000 people into this movement. He then confided in late 2016 that he wanted to work to reinvent Connecticut. I saw the wheels turning in his head—he was fired up to tackle not just the challenges that I personally faced, but the challenges that citizens and businesses of all sizes face across our state. Connecticut has immense natural beauty coupled with an innovative work force and community assets. Our strategic advantage, location between New York City and Boston, seems to have been left to wither for far too long. I know in my heart and mind, as Steve embarks on his journey to reinvent Connecticut, that our state stands a far better chance to keep businesses like ours and, frankly, the people I talk to every day, firmly planted in CT—especially if we are able to see his ideas and solutions put into action to create an economic reality and vibrant state we all want for our own families and children.

— Jeffrey Lederer
President, Prime Line

INTRODUCTION

I n *Run to the Fire,* Steve Obsitnik relates his experiences growing up in Connecticut during a period of thriving economic progress. Along with the lessons he learned along the way in the US Navy and as a technology entrepreneur and chief executive officer, it brings to life his values, vision and ideas to reinvent a Connecticut that has lost its way. The timing couldn't be more critical as Steve is a candidate for Governor of Connecticut. As I write this introduction to *Run to the Fire,* Connecticut needs new leadership and bold innovation now more than ever.

When I first came to Connecticut in 1965, it was a leading state in the country in terms of economic and personal opportunity. As Steve witnessed as a student at Stamford High School, several Fortune 500 companies were relocating to that city and others across Connecticut because of the high quality of life, proximity to large cities and good educational systems, but also because it was affordable (especially when there was no state income tax at the time).

Now, over fifty years later, career politicians in Connecticut have gotten us into a financial situation that leaves us with mounting deficit and debts. Meanwhile, the state is ranked as the second or third worst-run state in the nation across almost every metric. I read recently that $13 billion of taxable income has left the state in recent years (most of it has gone to Florida) along with the corporate loss of companies like General Electric and Aetna. This situation is directly attributable to how past politicians have made decisions to focus on growing state government rather than making Connecticut a place for businesses and families to thrive. Over one third of our state spending goes to paying for state pensions and healthcare along with debt service coverage as opposed to educating our youth and rebuilding our infrastructure.

Connecticut, essentially, is a big business, but for the past few decades the state has been poorly run. In my opinion, one of the main reasons for this performance is that none of our governors has ever run a company or organization before taking office. It goes without saying that Connecticut has big problems with outsized spending, deficits, looming debts and workforce size and compensation. A lot of corporations have dealt proactively with these same factors successfully and Connecticut needs someone with real business experience and judgment to turn around our state.

I have been around long enough to know the qualities that make for good business, government and philanthropic results. They are the same values and qualities that go into leadership: integrity, respect, discipline, responsibility and teamwork. That last quality is extremely important, because if you have a governor who can't develop a team, then he or she won't be able to enact real, long-term change.

In the time I have spent with Steve discussing the condition of our state and his ideas to improve it, he has demonstrated these important qualities. He has a strong reputation built on innovation and teamwork. The pages that follow give you an insight into the experiences and lessons that have shaped who Steve Obsitnik is today.

I believe the next leader of Connecticut must possess a business-oriented, leadership approach. Our state has an economy larger than most of the major corporations in this country. The people of Connecticut deserve someone who will focus on their well-being and keep their best interests in view. I believe that leader is Steve Obsitnik.

— Joel E. Smilow

Former Chairman & CEO, Playtex Products Inc.

Dedicated Philanthropist including the Smilow Cancer Hospital in New Haven, CT

Chapter 1

RUNNING SILENT, RUNNING DEEP

*It was early morning off the coast of Charleston, South Carolina, on board
a Sturgeon-class nuclear submarine. Above us, the June sky was a clear blue,
the water 78 degrees. Five miles out to sea, we dove deep, hundreds of feet
below the surface, the water turned dark and colder. Where we were going it
would be even deeper and darker, in waters 35 degrees and below.*

As an officer on board the USS *Ray*, my crewmates and I were
en route to the Arctic Circle. It was a mission of indetermi-
nate length. All we knew was that we'd be at sea for as long as
our food held out. Judging by the cases of canned fruit and vegetables
stacked in the passageways we were forced to walk on, we'd be gone a
very long time.

A few weeks into our deployment, I'd hit the rack at 2:30 a.m. after
standing watch, only to be awakened at 5:30 a.m. by the officer of
the deck on the IMC, the ship's intercom. He issued a call to general
quarters: "Fire! Engine room, lower level!," he barked.

Submariners are trained fire-fighters. A submarine can fill so
quickly with black smoke and toxic fumes that there can be little
chance of survival for anyone on board unless actions are taken quickly.
That is why we are trained to run toward fires—and all problems—not
away from them. Although this time it was only a drill, I sprinted
down to the engine room, donning my Emergency Air Breather, or

EAB, on the way. As the first officer on location, I took control and began assessing the situation in the lower level of the engine room. As a crewmate in the upper level was opening and closing the heavy hatch between the two engine rooms so I could share information, the hatch accidentally slipped from his grasp and struck me on the crown of my head. I fell down half a flight to the deck of the lower level engine room. At first, I was feeling okay and staggered to my feet, but blood quickly covered the mask of my EAB. Then everything went dark. I came to as the ship's medic was stitching up my scalp on a table in the officers' wardroom, a space normally reserved for meals and meetings but now turned into a makeshift clinic.

We were all brought back to reality when the officer of the deck came back on the IMC. "General quarters!," he shouted. "This is *not* a drill. Commence tracking target submarine." From long range, we had detected a Soviet Yankee-class submarine, and we began tracking it as we made our way farther north to execute our ultimate mission.

When a U.S. submarine leaves its home port, the Pentagon needs a way to know where it is at any point in time. To do this, the sub is assigned "boxes of water" that it must move between along its journey. Think of Tarzan, the King of the Jungle, following a planned route by jumping from one vine to the next. In a similar way, a submarine must move from one box of water to the next, each box defined by actual, physical coordinates that define an area of water in front and back, above and below it. As with Tarzan, the submarine is given a plan to move from box to box, or vine to vine. This lets officials in Washington know where that particular submarine is at any time without actually sending a message, thereby allowing it to remain hidden. Given the

highly secretive nature of our mission, that was of the utmost importance. The U.S. submarine force operates under a simple rule: If you
stay in your boxes, you are "operating to plan."

Just north of Norway, we handed off tracking of the Soviet sub to
another U.S. vessel. We moved into our next box of water, this time
entering the Arctic Circle, and eventually ending up under the polar
ice cap. The thickness of the ice in the Arctic is 12 to 15 feet on average,
but in places can extend to almost 70 feet, and now we were moving
beneath it. For this mission, when we weren't operating the submarine,
we were confined to our racks to keep as quiet as possible. Although the
machines and tools on board were rubber-coated, if someone were to
accidentally drop a hammer or a wrench, the noise could be heard many
miles away, potentially giving up our position and, possibly, our mission.

That mission? To find, identify and track another larger Soviet
submarine that would be testing a new and classified capability. Naval
Intelligence personnel and Navy Seals were on board to lend their
expertise. We'd received confirmation that somewhere inside a window of the next few weeks, the Soviets would be running a covert test
using this particular submarine. Our mission had come with one other
directive: don't get caught.

As we emerged from under the ice cap and entered the Barents and
Kara seas, we went into mission-mode. Initially, staying at periscope
depth some 50 feet below the surface, we were able to intercept information from the Soviet fleet, which had now come out in force to clear the
waters. They didn't want anyone to see what we were about to witness.

Finally, when the coast seemed clear, a huge Soviet submarine
appeared on the surface. We had to confirm that it was the actual

submarine before it submerged, so we dove and drew close. Our "mission moment" had arrived.

From the darkness of the ocean, we came up from under the Soviet sub, led by a spotlight that revealed the 10,000-ton hull of the submarine mere feet above us. The Soviets did not know we were there. With every crew member focused on the mission, we gathered video intelligence and, more importantly, an audio signature of the submarine's propeller, which is like a fingerprint. Once you have that information, you can identify that submarine anywhere in the ocean, kind of like tagging a sea lion. We had the right submarine and disappeared beneath it.

Shortly afterward, the Soviet submarine submerged and immediately executed a Cold War tactic called a "Crazy Ivan"—a classic Russian submarine movement involving a series of turns to clear the sub's baffles (the blind spot in the water directly behind a moving vessel) to ensure no submarine was hiding behind it. Fortunately, we had already gathered what we needed.

Hiding in our crucial box of water, we waited for what seemed like hours for the exercise to commence. Once again, the Soviet fleet "cleared the water" except for the USS *Ray*, which remained undetected. We came to periscope depth among over 20 ships and planes, as I recall, and successfully observed the secretive exercise. We then silently disappeared into the darkness of the sea, where our boxes of water guided us steadily and safely back home.

To this day, some 25 years later, the crew of the USS Ray cannot disclose the nature of the operation we surveilled. As important as the outcome, our "mission moment" defined what we as a crew could accomplish and were capable of achieving with discipline, preparation and teamwork.

LESSONS LEARNED

- Run toward the fire: Simply said, confront the crisis, don't shrink from it. You'll never gain control if you run away from the crisis.

- Prepare for the mission moment: There are few times in our lives when all the training and preparation that you do lead to a finite moment of importance. That moment on the battlefield, in business or in a personal challenge is the culmination of planning, execution and grit.

Chapter 2

THE FOUNDATIONS OF LEADERSHIP

My grandparents emigrated to America from both Western and Eastern Europe through Ellis Island. They brought with them their traditions, values and aspirations, along with a strong work ethic, that served as a foundation for my brothers and me to build upon. In effect, they imprinted their very lives on our characters and spirits. Reinforced by our parents, we always knew where we came from and also who we could become.

My father's parents, Michael and Suzanna Obsitnik, were Czechoslovakians and Byzantine Catholics who came to America in 1938. Their families lived in what is now the Slovak Republic, where they were mostly farmers. My grandfather, Michael, had come to the U.S. first, in 1928, and worked as a coal miner to earn enough money to move his new wife eventually here. He came to Western Pennsylvania, not far from Pittsburgh, and worked in the Heisley Mine #3 for eight years without once going back home. Suzanna remained in Czechoslovakia to take care of her parents. When he finally did return to Czechoslovakia, he tried to re-acclimate to life there, without success. My father, Vince, always told me that his dad never felt the same back in Czechoslovakia; he had worked as a farmer there and felt that life in America offered more opportunities than a lifetime in the fields. Two years after his return and following the birth of my dad, my grandfather had had enough and, as World War II inched closer, saw where life in Czechoslovakia was headed. He finally declared to my grandmother, "I can't make a living in the fields. There's no opportunity here. I'm going back to America." To this my grandmother replied, "You are not going this time without me." They immigrated to America together along with my father.

My grandmother had made the pivotal decision to move our family and its future to America. Six months before Hitler took over Czechoslovakia, they left the old country for good—a single decision that otherwise would have made my life and the life of my family very different. Together, Michael and Suzanna Obsitnik settled outside of Johnstown, PA, in the small, coal mining town of Nanty Glo. He went back into the Heisley mines until he contracted black lung disease from overexposure to coal dust. It was time to leave Western Pennsylvania. In Linden, New Jersey, where they had friends, both grandparents got jobs in the Karagheusian rug factory in Roselle Park, though work there was almost as environmentally dangerous as work in the coal mines with pervasive use of toxic chemicals. They worked opposite shifts so that one parent could be home with their four children. Eventually, they lost their jobs when the company moved south for cheaper labor. My grandmother found work in a cafeteria, however, and my grandfather got a job working for the City of Linden's road department. He was thrilled—he would finally be working outside in fresh air!

For my grandparents Michael and Suzanna, the path forward was straightforward: You went to bed early, you got up early, you put in a hard day's work and you did whatever you had to do for your family—at all costs. I am told this was particularly true of my grandfather. I never met him and have only seen one photograph of him. He was tall and wire-thin with piercing eyes behind dark-rimmed glasses. Although not formally educated, he was an avid reader and enjoyed talking politics.

The decisions my grandparents made in their lifetimes, and the courage to follow them, have served as examples for me my entire life. The age-old question, "If you could have dinner with anyone in history, who would it be?," is easy for me to answer: Michael Obsitnik.

My mother's parents, Arthur and Annemarie Harden, also left Europe, specifically Germany, to pursue the American Dream. Arthur emigrated in 1928 with $100 in his pocket and arrived months before the stock-market crash and the beginning of the Great Depression. He quickly got a job at Merck Pharmaceuticals, but his lack of English proved an impediment, and he was let go. Instead, he started a business with his friend, Erwin Fritching. Erwin's wife had invited her sister, Annemarie Manns, to visit the U.S., where she met my grandfather, and the two of them began what turned into a transatlantic relationship over the next year. They would write letters back and forth to each other. In one letter, Arthur wrote asking her to move to America to be with him. My grandmother's response was, "Come to Germany, ask my father for permission, and after we marry I will go to the United States." He returned to Germany to do just that. They left Germany shortly after marrying. On their exit, the German government confiscated my grandmother's German passport and, for a period of time, she had no country.

Ultimately, in starting his own business, my maternal grandfather wanted to control his own destiny, and, in this country, he envisioned the possibilities for doing just that. Like many Germans, he and a long-time partner started a precision-machine shop, bought a few drill presses and lathes and began turning out small machinery parts to sell.

My grandfather Arthur was a soft-spoken man who led by example. I spent summer days working with him in his office at American Products, the precision-machinery parts company he founded in Union, New Jersey. My summer job, which I began at an early age, was sharpening his Ticonderoga #2 pencils, a brand that I still use today as a reminder of him. As I got older, I was allowed to sweep the shop floor and observe the master craftsmen, who once in a while let me work the machines. I loved going onto the machine-shop floor and smelling the fragments of freshly drilled metal falling away from the lathe while the workers—most of them Europeans who had also immigrated here for a better life—focused on the orders at hand at their stations. The highlight of the week was Friday at noon when my grandfather would take me with him to Oscar's Restaurant, a German place that served authentic bratwurst. Many of the American Products employees would gather there for lunch, drink a beer or two and watch soccer games.

At the end of the day, my grandfather would say, "Okay, here's your dollar." On my first day of work, as I went to take the bill, he pulled it back and said, "Oh, no. Part of it goes to taxes, and part of it goes to charity, so you get the 40 cents that's left." I was stunned. "*What?*" I remember saying. "Where did it go?" And he said, "Now you realize where your money goes and what you have to take care of." He didn't like paying taxes, but he did recognize that you have to take care of people. He then would talk about the importance of saving rather than spending, thereby teaching me the meaning of deferred gratification, "There is a reason that dessert comes at the end of the meal," he'd say.

"It is the same with life. Work hard and enjoy the results at the end of the meal."

My grandfather Arthur lived his entire life by these principles. He was the hardest-working and most selfless person I knew. Although my grandmother called him by his nickname, Stumpis, which means "little stump" in German, he had the heart of a lion. He didn't know what pain meant. He walked around with a hernia for four years before the pain finally informed him that it was worth missing work to have it operated on. In 1981, the epitome of his career came when he and his partner, Walter Eickeley, were invited to the White House to receive the award for the Best Small Business Sub Contractor in America from President Ronald Reagan in the Rose Garden. I think it was the first time I ever saw my grandfather really stop and enjoy the moment. Only death, at the age of 99, slowed him down. It shows what a beer-and-beef diet can do!

Both sets of grandparents quickly assimilated to life in the New World, understanding what it took to get, find or create a job and make money, and they both grasped that the road to success lay not just in hard work but in education. Both shared similar values, ethics and family principles. Both represent what this country has done and can do for families. Both sets of grandparents fought their way into the middle class through hard work and seeing that their kids were educated. When I was a kid, I appreciated their sacrifices but have come to understand more clearly their own grit and determination. My dad's parents worked hard at manual jobs that took their toll. Meanwhile, my mom's parents fought to build a business from the ground up, one customer at a time. Although they pursued slightly different paths, they both shared a vision and desire to create a better life.

From my grandfathers, I received two distinctly different images and messages, though both taught me the value of dedication, hard work and devotion to family. But in a way, it was my immigrant grandmothers who most encouraged me to forge my path in life.

They were remarkable women—forces of nature! Both immigrants from different countries in Europe, they found themselves living 15 minutes apart in New Jersey. They loved that state and what New York City had to offer. My paternal grandma, Suzanna, went around in a babushka; grew and pickled everything; taught us Slovak (to this day, I can still sing "It's a Small World" in Slovak!); and was simple but wise in her own special way.

Suzanna went by the Slovak name for grandma—"Baba." After losing my grandfather in the 1958, she continued to work two to three jobs at a time to support her family. My dad once told me, "We really had to raise ourselves because Baba had to work. We figured out how to cook for ourselves and get to school." Early on, she made clear that to us the importance of the religion we were to be raised in and how we should treat people. She imparted how to do the simple things in life too. You rolled your stuffed cabbage and filled your pierogi *this* way! But she loved us to a remarkable degree and knew when to be patient, which I grew to appreciate as I got older and would come up from college to visit her. She was a very practical woman. As kids, when we inevitably got a cut or bruise as kids, she would wrap it in cold bacon (who knew?). The church was a big part of her spiritual and social life. She helped to clean the church and was one of the people before Mass every Sunday who recited the rosary. She was proud of her own children and what they became. As a single mother after the loss of my grandfather, she singlehandedly saw that my father and his brother, my Uncle Mike, attended the U.S. Naval Academy, and that my Aunt Menkie and Uncle Tom both graduated from Rutgers University. Her protective reach extended to me and my brothers as well. My brother, Paul, and I once visited her in Iselin, NJ, while we were on break from the Naval Academy. We took her to church dressed in our uniforms, which I can assure you was not our idea. I still remember the look on her face and the pride in her voice when we entered church as her friends lit up with shared pride for her.

Baba was hands-on across all aspects of life. She may not have been able to help with math or literary references, but when it came to relationships she had a keen read of human nature. When my brothers and I began dating, she wanted to make sure we found the right women. Her advice to us, famous within the family, was this: "Look, you keep the one you have and look for a better one at the same time—until you get married! Then you're done." She was nothing if not pragmatic, a trait that in many ways extends to me. Years later, my aunt told that me that Baba said of my wife, Suzanne Tager, "Suzanne is the right person for Steve." Glad I followed her advice and found the right one. (In hindsight, this may have been a little protective, but she was dedicated to us!)

My maternal grandmother, Annemarie, went by the German name for grandmother, "Oma." She, too, was a strong woman. She was well read and loved to travel. She was also the first one of all my friends and brothers to buy the Bruce Springsteen album *Born in the U.S.A.* My grandmother lit up every room she entered and drove the conversation. For 45 years, she did yoga every morning before most of us knew what it was, and she was more flexible at 90 than I was at 35. But she was no hippy-dippy grandmother; yoga for her was more about health and longevity than about show. She worked at it, as she did with everything, to accomplish something, and she instilled in me the same standard.

Other than keeping my back in check, the reason I do yoga now is probably because of her, and the reason I became a good sailor was absolutely because of her. When, at first, I balked at the activity, finding it boring, she both objected to my objections and made me feel good about my efforts. She applied enough pressure to make me aware of my strengths and opportunities. As a kid, I would spend a few days every visit in the summer racing Sunfish sailboats against kids who did it every day on the Jersey Shore. Well, I finally won one of these meaning-less races, which at the time felt like the America's Cup. Racing to my grandmother's home on my bicycle, I got a shoelace caught up in the gears, which threw me from the bike. I finally reached her home with bleeding elbows and knees but with a first-place ribbon that I handed to her. Oma looked me over and said, "I guess you really wanted to win, but I didn't think sailing was a contact sport."

My grandmother, Oma, had more influence in steering me toward my path in life than I think she realized. With me, she seemed to have an especially prescient sense of my potential and a savvy way of draw-ing that out. Although she challenged my reasons for going to the Naval Academy, she planted a seed inside me early on, "You know, I see something different in you. I see these businessmen and politicians out there talking about serving others, but you care about people, you're good with people, you're smart, you're honest. If any of the brothers are going to do anything, it's going to be you." I have a feeling now that she probably said this to all my brothers!

In hindsight, I think that all of these early experiences gave me and my brothers a foundation and a support system that are fundamental to most people's success in life, certainly to mine. It just took a little while for me to understand their importance.

That realization came in 2012 in Bridgeport when I was running for the U.S. Congress. One weekday, I paid a visit to the pastor of a large congregation in Bridgeport following his sermon the previous Sunday. "I had difficulty fully understanding your sermon last week, Reverend," I said. "In talking about the challenges within your congregation, you talked about how you want young people to be educated and be entrepreneurs. I get that. But then you threw in that government has to help in the end." And, I went on, "Given my background, I don't know how government and entrepreneurship can be held in one hand—they are often antithetical ideas." The Reverend looked at me for what seemed like a long moment, then finally said, "Tell me about your grandparents and parents," and when I did, he said, "Well, a lot of kids here don't have that foundation or support. You've had support for generations to the point that you don't even see it anymore. My community doesn't. Government is necessary in many cases to replace that support network."

Whereas I disagreed that government is the solution, I understood the Reverend's point. Our conversation, many years after my grandparents had passed, made me realize that these gifts—encouragement and challenge and accountability and responsibility—accrue over time, down the generations. These gifts are all the things that people who love you do, because they love and believe in you and that make you stronger, so that when you leave the house you're able to go out and compete in a world that is fiercely, and increasingly, competitive.

Something else of great value bequeathed to us down the generations were my grandparents' and parents' expectations for me and my brothers. These high expectations drove me and still do. When I think about this, I am not sure if it is a fear of personal failure or a fear of not being able to live up to their expectations for me. But also mixed with those feelings is an early fear that if I didn't get a good education, and if I didn't continually challenge myself, I could end up working a job and having a life I didn't necessarily want. At the same time, there was proof in my grandparent's experiences that I could take risks and *create* a job if I wanted!

Regardless, I believe personal thoughts of doubt and failure must be treated almost as a mental cancer, and you have to work hard to shrink them from your mind. With my children, in this ever-more competitive world, I try to get them to reach their own potential, using their own curiosity and drive. I try to relieve a bit of the pressures of high school by getting them to focus on the end, not the means; telling them that although I was very lucky to attend and work hard in great schools, there are many more successful people who did not get the training I did. Chart your own path, I tell them, execute well and don't lie, cheat or steal along the way. Life will surprise you.

In my life, there has been undeniable proof that the timing of my brothers' and my coming of age in a country like the United States was fortuitous. Two experiences in particular when I was still young bring home what being an American meant to my grandparents and to me.

I don't recall hearing my maternal grandparents talk much about life in Germany; they kept their memories of leaving that country for America and World War II mostly to themselves. My grandfather was a fierce supporter of the U.S. automobile industry, and he championed how America was leading the industrial world. He and my grandmother looked forward to and ingrained in us a sense of the magnitude of the opportunity we now had. Still, when I was a teenager, they and my mother took me and my brother, Jim, to West Germany to meet our distant relatives and understand our roots. I had really wanted to meet my great-grandfather who lived to 99 years of age, but he passed away nine months before our visit.

On the trip, we visited many of my grandparents' siblings and relatives, and toured a brewery a cousin ran and a ceramics factory operated by another relative that turned out "blue gray" pottery. These were industrious, creative, imaginative and entrepreneurial people! The debates I remember having with them centered on which country had better roads and automobiles, although I think everyone agreed that German beer had a leg up on U.S. brands at the time. Then, in 1983 when I was 16, my Dad took Jim, my brother, and me to Czechoslovakia.

The differences were stark. In democratic West Germany, most of my mother's relatives spoke at least decent English. In communist Czechoslovakia, on the other hand, no one really did. And yet language didn't matter. My father's relatives took us out into the fields with them. They were so excited to have us there that they dug up a bottle of home-made vodka—that had been buried in the ground fermenting for five years. To a 16-year-old, it tasted like paint thinner. They had us work in the fields and milk the cows. For supper, they had me cut the head off a chicken and, against my better judgment, I tried but it slipped between my legs. I can't honestly describe the situation, but needless to say, I know what the old saying, "like a chicken with its head cut off," means all too well.

Though my relatives seemed happy enough to me at the time— again, this was in the early-'80s—there was an important lesson to be gleaned from their lives. Getting to know my family there made me see that that's what my life might have been like: I would have been tilling the fields, hearing stories of the Communists repressing their freedom of speech and religion. That trip, more than any in my life, showed me what my grandparents had endured and why they emigrated to America. In reality, many people in communist Czechoslovakia wanted a democratic form of government. Before we left, an eight-year-old second cousin came up to my father and said something in Slovak. When I asked what she'd said, my father translated it as "I would like to hide in your suitcase and come to America to live."

From there, I was curious to visit one more country. When we were planning our trip to Czechoslovakia, I looked at the map and saw how close we would be to the Soviet Union. I said to my dad, "Why don't we continue on and visit Russia?" That's exactly what we did. From Czechoslovakia, we took a train to Kiev, Ukraine, and stayed there for a few days. From Kiev, we flew to Moscow, the center of the Soviet Union and Communism. In Moscow, we saw bread lines, and I felt a palpable heaviness in the air. People would walk up to us on the street to ask if they could feel our Levi jeans and offer to buy our cameras. I felt they wanted to experience in some way the freedom we, as Americans, embodied and that they had read about. Walking in Red Square under what appeared to be the oversight of Soviet soldiers, and having to check in daily with the hotel on our return, left a tangible feeling of oppression and control. When we got on the plane on our return trip to the U.S. and the pilot spoke over the intercom to announce that we'd finally left Soviet airspace, everyone broke out in applause. This was more than just a trip to Europe.

The message from those journeys to the old countries was clear: We, as citizens of the greatest democracy in history, can choose the direction we want our country and lives to go in, and we can do it by electing the right leaders. We can leave the road to ruin for the road to prosperity. It is something that is possible. Germany has now been unified and people in the Czech Republic and Slovak Republic live in democracy and are much happier and more prosperous because of it. All it demands is that someone be willing to stand up and say, "We've been going down the wrong road and need to change." Then, it's just a matter of convincing enough people that there is, in fact, a better road to take.

As history repeats itself, states and nations must constantly look to challenge the status quo for a better path for their people.

LESSONS LEARNED

- Choose a path for your family: The courage to make decisions that are right for a person and a family set in place unknown benefits and yield opportunities for generations to follow.

- Defer gratification: I learned from my grandparents to work hard, be a good person, trust in myself and strive to keep dessert where it is meant to be—at the end of the meal, not at the beginning.

Chapter 3

ROLE MODELS AT HOME

It is hard to capture all the ways that parents help us along life's journey from cradle to adulthood. I can simply say that the best decision I ever made was picking my parents! That set in motion so many events that have shaped my life.

Like me, my father, Vince, was stationed in New London as a young lieutenant in the Navy. He was there in the early 1960s. One day he got call from his high school friend, Jack Paterno.

"Vince, I met the perfect person for you last week," Jack said.

"Tell me about her," my Dad said.

"Her name is Annemarie Harden, and she's down the road from you at Connecticut College. Her family is from New Jersey, too."

"You know, I go to sea a lot, Jack. It's probably not a good time."

After Jack's persistence, my father agreed to meet her.

Two weeks later, he went to her dormitory at Connecticut College to pick her up for a date. Dad remembers that moment vividly.

"I waited at the bottom as your mother floated down the stairs wearing a black skirt with knee-high socks and a white blouse. My heart was immediately taken."

When I've asked him what really made him want to marry my mother, beyond the predictable things he mentioned, one stood out: "I knew that I wanted to accomplish a lot in my family and personal life," he said, "and I needed someone who was going to be a smart, thoughtful and independent partner."

That captures my mother well. To me, she is the model of kindness, dedication, hard work and, simply, unconditional love. When we moved to Stamford in 1979, I was miserable after I got there. Starting at a new school (Turn of River Middle School) wasn't an easy step. I was a decent soccer player back then, and the quality of play, unlike today, was not very high. But my mother knew that once I got placed on a team, it would turn me around. She searched to find the only travel-soccer team at the time in Stamford and placed a call to Mr. Ortega, who coached the team. As she recalls, the conversation went something like this:

"Mr. Ortega, we moved here a few months ago, and I would like my son to try out for the team."

"I'm sorry, Mrs. … Obsitnik, is it? … but tryouts are over. Your son will have to wait until next season."

"You don't understand. He's a pretty good player, and I need to do something to help make this move successful for him."

"Well, okay," Mr. Ortega relented. "Have him come to practice tomorrow, but I'm not promising anything."

"Will do," my mother said. "You won't regret it." In fact, the only thing anyone should have regretted was if Coach Ortega did not give in to her.

After a long practice in the rain on a cold, dreary day in October, my mother got a call that evening from Coach.

"You weren't kidding, Mrs. Obsitnik," he said, "your son is great."

"So, I guess he made the team," was all my mother said and all she wanted to hear!

I went on to captain the Stamford Shamrocks, alongside Coach Ortega's son, Kevin, for many years to follow.

That was just one example of how my mother has always been exceptional at helping my brothers and me forge a path forward.

My father, for his part, has always been the standard bearer of our family. From an early age, he had to assume that role when he lost his father. He has always set a high standard for me and my brothers. In the early years, discipline was a key theme of his. We went to church every Sunday at 8 a.m., and he would comb our hair with sugar water that gave it the texture of rock candy—not a single hair would be out of place! My dad is the person who taught me that there is something more important than your own self-interests. Belief in God, family and country are the key tenets he instilled in me and my brothers. To this day, he is the role model I look to as an example of hard work, family-orientation, dedication and persistence.

I have learned a lot from my parents, especially how hard it can be to hold back advice when trying to steer our kids away from rocky shores. My parents really let each of us kids follow our own paths with all the love and support they could muster. I've also learned from my parents that the role you play in your kids' lives changes. My parents over time added the roles of coaches, mentors and friends as they continued to impact my life.

After they married in 1961, my parents settled in Connecticut because my dad was stationed on the USS *Blenny*, a Balao-class submarine. My mother went to work as an elementary-school teacher in Waterford, Connecticut, and together they lived in officers housing in Groton.

Over time, my parents raised four boys: Vince, Paul, Steve and Jim—all named after saints, to my grandmother Baba's relief and happiness. Just as my paternal and maternal grandparents had laid the foundation for their children to thrive and succeed in life, so too my parents prepared my brothers and me for the lives and careers we were to have. They instilled certain values and a code of conduct that served as guideposts for how we interacted with them and with one another growing up. These included the importance of family, religion, work, education and individual responsibility. Ronald Reagan once said, "The family has always been the cornerstone of American society. Our families nurture, preserve and pass on to each succeeding generation the values we share and cherish, values that are the foundation of our freedoms." By this standard, my parents did more than their fair share.

We four boys grew up in a supportive environment, and we worked well together, despite the natural and healthy competition that occurs among brothers and the marked differences in our personalities. Summer camp for us was being pushed into our backyard to create our own fun. Early on, when I was in elementary school, we all shared a paper route. We delivered papers by bicycle—with the exceptional few times when one of our parents drove us on the route in the family Pontiac station wagon because of snow or rain. All four of us were also altar boys at Saint John the Baptist Church in Trumbull, which at the time was the only Byzantine Catholic church in the area.

Education was also important. My mother, the elementary-school teacher, managed the homework process and challenged us. She would never do the work but instead would share a few clues or explain principles to get us to figure out the problem. I had the most difficult time learning the multiplication tables. She was the one who spent hours with me, not letting me memorize them, but internalizing them with practical examples what was actually happening with the numbers.

Although I lagged in math when I was young, her efforts gave me an enormous boost in confidence.

Mom was a traditional housewife, and she went the extra mile in whatever she did—even cutting and sewing Shamrocks to the Stamford Shamrocks soccer team uniforms back in the day! She was in constant motion—she still is—cooking, cleaning, ironing. We call her "The Perpetual Motion Machine." Simply said, she is incredibly talented with a lot of energy. If she were born today, with the opportunities that are more available to women than they were back then, she might still choose to raise her family, but she also could have created a career outside the home that would probably exceed what I've been able to accomplish.

Dad had an engineering mindset and introduced technology into his sons' lives. He brought home the first electric typewriter, the first IBM personal computer, the first video game of the day (Larry Bird versus Dr. J, I believe). We were fortunate to have an early view of technological innovations, yet I think we only understood a fraction of the change that was coming to the world.

Each one of my brothers has also had a unique influence on me. Although similar in many ways, their influence on me differed in many other ways.

Vince, being the oldest, was smart and quiet, rarely raising his voice and above the rivalry of his siblings. He simply created his own path. Vince was, and remains, very entrepreneurial. He started what turned into a lucrative landscaping service while he was still in high school, training us and overseeing the jobs. A savvy businessman, he took a cut of the profits for his "overhead"—even when he wasn't on site. Our grandfather, Opa, was probably advising him! Vince eventually recruited Paul, me and Jim to help, and when he and Paul went off to college, Jim and I took over the business, which we ran while in high school. Vince is a veterinarian with multiple locations, a testament to his early business acumen. When I asked him why he picked Peachtree City, Georgia, for his practices, he simply said, "I went to the U.S. Census data and picked an area that was growing fast and a good place to raise a family." Common sense he was not short on. There are two things I am particularly mindful of regarding Vince's impact on me. First, as the oldest, he was the first to protect us from neighborhood bullies. Second, he has always been good at taking calculated risks—but he does take risks.

Paul, second in line, was the family daredevil and outspoken free-thinker with clever wit. He was also probably the smartest one of the litter, academically speaking, but lacked common sense at times. One time, I remember, I walked into his room and found him standing in front of an open window on the second floor of our house in Stamford.

"What are you doing?" I asked.

"Oh," Paul said matter-of-factly, "I'm going to jump out the window."

But why, I wanted to know.

"Because I can," he said.

With that, he climbed out and dangled from the window sill. Observing our mother vacuuming in the room directly below his, however, and not wanting to alarm her with the sight of her son sailing past the dining-room window, he climbed back in. A few minutes later, as Mom moved into another room, he jumped. I stuck my head out the window and watched as he hit the ground and did a forward somersault.

"Why did you do that?" I called down.

"I wanted to break my fall by transferring the kinetic energy from the fall to the roll," he calmly explained. Paul was probably 15 years old, and already thinking like the engineer he eventually would be. I had no idea what he was saying at the time. Paul blazed a path for me at Annapolis, the submarine force and Silicon Valley. He has dedicated his career to the computer-networking space with companies like 3Com, Williams and Juniper. I have always viewed Paul as my "gold standard" to achieving results in school, the Navy and business. He sets a high bar for himself, and that has made me a better person.

My youngest brother is Jim. He probably got the best attributes of all of us; that or, maybe, the youngest is able to watch before doing, so that gives them a leg up. Jim was the best athlete, student and friend all wrapped into one. Because of our ages, we tended to do more things together. There is little motivation more powerful than your younger brother nipping at your heels. And he nipped pretty good. He was and remains the one willing to try new things, such as moving to Japan after college to learn a language and a culture to putting himself out there as a performer, things I probably could not do. We had our own venture when we were 9 and 11, respectively. We created a family news-paper called, I think, *The Obsitnik Times*. In it was family news from our extended family, and we created crossword puzzles and games. We hand-wrote the editions—this was before our Dad brought home one of the early IBM Selectric typewriters—and we sold subscriptions to our aunts and uncles. Jim has gone on to an impressive career in Silicon Valley as well. He has worked with some of the best companies in tech-nology, including Netscape, Commerce One, Dell and Oracle. He has long surpassed nipping at my heels. From Jim, I try to internalize the old saying, "Don't sweat the small stuff. And it is all small." He keeps a fresh, easy-going perspective on life that is infectious.

As for myself, I felt I had to constantly work harder than my brothers to keep pace with them. Part of this may have been due to the eye problem I had at birth. Reading was a difficult act for me growing up. The other part is that my brothers are just good, smart, hardworking people who have done well on their own. Ralph Waldo Emerson may have had it right when he said, "Every (person) I meet is my superior in some way. In that I learn from him." In the end, measuring ourselves against one another simply raised the bar for accomplishment in the family and made us all better people persons—sons, brothers, husbands and fathers.

Together, our parents' sense of partnership and the environment they created for us four boys allowed us grow in our own direction and use their relationship as a role model for our own families today. I see now how my relationship with my wife, Suzanne, reflects my parents' true partnership and love. In turn, we strive to pass these gifts on to our daughters and, hopefully, to everyone we meet and serve.

LESSONS LEARNED

- Challenging yet supportive environments allow people to develop at their own rate to achieve their potential.

- Open yourself to watching and listening to others around you: Everyone has something to teach you.

- Ronald Reagan once said, "The family has always been the cornerstone of American society. Our families nurture, preserve and pass on to each succeeding generation the values we share and cherish."

Chapter 4

STAMFORD, THE CITY THAT WORKED FOR A KID

One afternoon in the fall of 2017 as I was in my car listening to the radio, a song came on by Blues Traveler that captured me. John Popper, the band's lead singer, grew up in Stamford at the same time I did. Although I didn't know him, his song "Back in the Day" immediately transported me to that time and place:

"It's been a while since I've left home
But I'm coming on back today,
Kinda funny but I picture it only
Exactly as it was back in the day.
Sure enough when the train pulls in
There's so little that I recognize.
Is it the scenery or my selective memory
Or just a simple fact that I gotta realize?
My friends have gone and their lives have moved on
And I guess that's just the way it is.
If this town has grown beyond my home
I guess it all comes down to this.
I close my eyes and feel like it was back in the day
But those times have long been through.
The dying of the light is gone

But it's back in the day
Like a wish that comes half true."
"Back in the Day" by Blues Traveler

Connecticut enjoyed a national reputation as a vibrant place in which to raise children and pursue careers in many well-paying industries. At least that was the case in the 1970s and '80s when I came of age in Stamford. The city's slogan was simple: "Stamford: The City That Works." And, it worked in many ways—from the school system, which was a draw for young families like mine, to the business climate, thanks to leaders who championed innovation, risk taking and growth. Stamford was the gateway to Connecticut, as well as New England.

Then, as now, geography played a key role in the state's appeal. It was our proximity to New York City and Boston, plus local advantages over these areas, that attracted people: Connecticut boasted quality K-12 school systems and centers of higher education across the state, and commerce hubs from finance and insurance to manufacturing. Our low taxes attracted people, and we had solid infrastructure and reliable transportation. Connecticut also offered an attractive quality of life— beaches, lakes and rivers; forests, parks and farms; small but vibrant downtowns with great restaurants and cultural institutions like the Rich Forum in Stamford, the highly-regarded Westport Country Playhouse, New Haven's Long Wharf Theatre and more. There was an energy to the state's cities and towns that called to companies and to families like mine.

In short, Connecticut had all the things that people could possibly want in a state. The same feeling that people have today when they move to Boston, Austin or Nashville conjures up the feelings I had back then. Life in Connecticut was good for many in those days, and people were moving in.

In 1979, my parents moved to Stamford at the same time that IBM and other major corporations were relocating other families to the area. General Electric had moved from New York to Fairfield, Connecticut, just five years earlier with the help of real-estate entrepreneurs like Bill Raveis. When I asked Bill what it was like to do business then, he said, "It was incredible. Everyone wanted to move here because of the location and advantages. And we moved all the large corporations in." If memory serves me, I believe Stamford had one of the highest concentrations of Fortune 500 companies—including American Can, GTE, Xerox, Singer and Pitney Bowes—of any city in America. If you compared it to similar cities of its size, which at the time contained approximately 100,000 people, it was the Fortune 500 capital of America. Even in high school, as we drove around town, I felt their corporate presence and noticed the logos of great brands adorning the streets of Stamford. Years later, I read a quote from business thinker and author Peter Drucker that put this memory into perspective: "Whenever you see a successful business," he wrote, "someone once made a courageous decision." And people were making a lot of courageous decisions to come to Stamford.

Downtown, tower cranes stretched their necks high into the sky. New office buildings and condominiums were rising and new restaurants opening. Frank and Robert Rich, pioneering Stamford contractors with a vision of what their city could become, created a new city skyline as the chosen developers of a massive urban-renewal project downtown. Hiring famous architects like César Pelli, in the late 1970s and early-'80s, the Rich brothers built the Stamford Marriott Hotel and the Stamford Town Center Regional Mall, the first of its size and quality in Fairfield and Westchester counties.

Along with the Riches, politicians like Tom Meskill and Ella Grasso, who both governed the state consecutively from 1971 through 1980, and Stewart B. McKinney, the Republican Congressman who represented the Fourth Congressional District from 1971 to 1987, had a keen understanding of the state's advantages and how to attract newcomers—residents and businesses alike. In a 1984 *New York Times* article entitled "Connecticut's Economy Is Now One of the Best in U.S.," author Tom Lueck wrote, "Small, technologically advanced companies are moving in to replace brass mills, textile plants and other outdated factories. At the same time, businesses are opening almost daily to support new corporate office complexes in Stamford, Hartford and other Connecticut cities. … Sparked by the growth of high-technology companies around Boston and a rapidly expanding demand for business services, the experts contend, the entire region, particularly Connecticut and Massachusetts, is experiencing something akin to an economic "renaissance."

This is the Stamford—this is the Connecticut—I grew up in.

It isn't surprising that Connecticut exuded a drive to design and build something new—in many cases from nothing. That kind of rigor was woven into the very fabric of the state. Today it remains in our DNA, waiting for a chance to re-emerge. And examples of hope exist, like the development of Harbor Point in Stamford fighting to attract Millennials and businesses back to that city.

From its very beginnings, Connecticut prospered as a haven for scholars, innovators, inventors and entrepreneurs—first as an agricultural and trading power, then as a leader in manufacturing during and after the Civil War and the Industrial Revolution. In everything from arms, tools, clocks and aviation to textiles, insurance and financial services, Connecticut made history and was world-renowned for "firsts" across a broad spectrum of interests and disciplines.

"Yankee ingenuity" was a phrase no doubt minted from the early fires of industriousness. Invented here were many of the nation's, and the world's, firsts: The first public library (New Haven); newspaper *(Hartford Courant)*; dictionary (authored by Hartford native Noah Webster); law school (Litchfield); medical diploma (Yale); insurance company (ITT Hartford Group in "the insurance capital of the world"); cotton gin (invented and manufactured in Connecticut by Eli Whitney); mass-produced revolver (invented and manufactured by Hartford native Samuel Colt); helicopter (designed by immigrant Igor Sikorsky at his plant in Stratford); patented can opener (invented by Waterbury resident Ezra Warner); spring-click tape measurer (invented by Alvin J. Fellows of New Haven); factory town (Seymour), and, of personal importance to me, nuclear submarine USS *Nautilus* (based in New London). Over time, these visionaries also created thousands of jobs for Connecticut citizens.

I see now that growing up in Connecticut in the early 1980s had a large impact on my development. Being surrounded by high-quality companies and the influx of people was a good thing because the people in my life beyond my family shaped my perspective. I can't help but think that some of that leadership spirit and entrepreneurial drive that I have worked so hard to develop was planted and nurtured during my years at Stamford High School.

What I didn't know at the time but learned many years later was that Stamford was a highly segregated town. I was unaware of this because my school had become integrated, and I was friends with a wide mix of people. A volunteer-citizen committee came together in

Stamford in the early '70s around the fact that three of the 12 elementary schools were 90 percent or more African-American, and all were downtown. As Mort Lowenthal, chairman of the group, recalled, "All the rest were all white, and many of us thought that changing this would make our city and country a better place."

I met Mort in 2011. After a long conversation, I came to realize that he and this citizen-led group changed my generation and many more to follow. Lowenthal's group studied the problem and recommended a full integration of Stamford schools, starting with the elementary schools. Once presented to and studied by the Stamford Board of Education, their recommendations were adopted. In fact, as Mort recalls, "Stamford was probably the first city in the country to integrate its elementary schools."

How did this citizen-powered effort affect me? My two older brothers, Vince and Paul, attended Rippowam High School in the middle of town. By the time I was ready to go to high school, followed eventually by my younger brother, Jim, we were bused to Stamford High. As a result of that plan, I went from going to a school with a majority of white students to one that was made up of minorities—roughly 50 percent African-American and Latino.

In addition, there was a diversity of parents. Some had white-collar jobs; many others were in the Stamford fire or police departments; some were even in prison. I also had friends who had recently immigrated to the U.S. from Iran and India. It was a true mosaic of America, and that was a good thing. Learning in this environment really opened my eyes to experiencing a broader world and exposed me to other perspectives that, up until that point, I hadn't understood. It also gave me an awareness of how empathy and understanding can strengthen and benefit a community. It was the best education in diversity.

The school soccer team, which I captained in my senior year, took up most of my time out of school and was made up of kids who were Greek, Italian, Jewish, Latino, African-American and even a Byzantine Catholic—me. Some of the best life- lessons happened on the upper field at Stamford High. I vividly remember Frank Pereira, who was our leading goal scorer. He had many of the physical traits of the New York Cosmos' Giorgio Chinaglia. Italian, tall, fast and strong, he took more than his fair share of shots on goal as the center forward or striker. I once asked him, "Frank, you miss so many of your shots on goal, why don't you pass it to someone else who may have a better shot?" He simply responded, "You can't score if you don't shoot." His answer may not have been the epitome of teamwork, but years later I internalized that to mean that each chance in life is an individual shot at success. If you never take the shot, the ball doesn't have a chance at going in. We all have to take risks and step out of our comfort zones to achieve great things. Whether it's finally passing the P2 exam for your plumbing license, earning your degree, starting a business or asking that special person to marry you, the ball will never have a chance of going in the net if you don't take the shot.

Although I and my core group of friends fancied ourselves "athletes," we were more student-athletes, with the emphasis on "student." This was probably wise, as none of us would have survived as athletes past the high-school level. Of that bigger group, there were three people who influenced me in very different ways. Bill Samers by far has been the most complicated and positive influence on my life. *He* could write a book! He was infinitely curious and challenging, and the older I get the more I like and admire those qualities in people.

After graduating from high school with a 1.90 average, Bill went on to become an accomplished lawyer and currently works for the UJA Federation of New York.

Another friend, Jason Sheftell, was the creative one who, over time, opted not to pursue a corporate career path in order to chase his dream of being the next Ernest Hemingway. Jason was obsessed with exploring cultures and why people are who they are. Even back then, he would take us into downtown Stamford's housing project, Southfield Village—referred to as "The V"—to understand other parts of Stamford. Doug Fuchs, meanwhile, was the most focused amongst us. He always had a clear vision of his goals and what was needed to accomplish them. He was also the basketball player among us and often took us with him to Haig Avenue to grab a pickup game, though my eye problems definitely didn't make me the standout player. We also spent a lot of time together hanging out and debating at Mario's Pizza on High Ridge Road. We talked a lot about the future and our goals and ambitions. We shared many similar values, among them frugality, hard work and challenging the assumptions of life. We would find our-selves rolling from one of our homes to the next, each with a different feeling yet with a similar and welcoming environment.

Our generation grew up at an awkward time in our country's history. We followed the baby boomers, who questioned many of our institutions and laws. We were Generation X or, less generously, "The Lost Generation" of latchkey kids. Families increasingly had two parents working, and this had an effect on how kids grew up. It was the post-Vietnam era and also the decade of Wall Street greed, most evidently portrayed by Michael Douglas' character, Gordon Gekko, in *Wall Street*. That movie had a profound influence on many of us, the blind ambition of making money permeating our culture. But what I remember is Bill and Doug needling me when I started to focus on attending the U.S. Naval Academy for college.

"Why would you want to serve in the military for nine years?," they grilled me. "Don't you want to succeed? You could have a lucrative career as a lawyer or investment banker."

The questions lingered for a long time. I have to say I did feel a bit different because of my choices. I am sure Bill and Doug are still questioning my career decisions! As it turned out, Doug went on to serve as an Assistant U.S. Attorney. Bill, as I mentioned, is a lawyer for the UJA Federation. Jason took a different tack, given his literary mind, but he encouraged me to listen to my gut. He became a successful *New York Post* journalist yet unfortunately died a few years ago. Generation X is now followed by Generation Y or Millennials, who rightfully raise more questions than we did about social justice and their desire to give back to society. Jason, who was ahead of his time, embodied this questioning attitude and that made me a better person. In hindsight, all four of us did went on to serve a larger purpose than what had been foreshadowed by the egocentric 1980s.

There are times in our childhood when we can vividly remember exactly where we were. One of those times for me was the shooting of President Ronald Reagan in March of 1981. I had just gotten off the bus and walked into my house. My mom had gone with my father on a business trip, and Baba, my dad's mother, was there in front of the television in tears. We sat there with my brothers for the next few hours, watching the live broadcast. She recounted the same feeling she had when John F. Kennedy was shot. It was yet another example of her love for this country and the opportunities it gave her kids.

Some of the smallest events in our childhoods can also play a big part in our lives. I remember one of the first times I went to Bill Samer's house, which his father, Bernie, had designed in his spare time—Doug Fuchs facetiously referred to him as Frank Lloyd Samers. It was for a break-fast following either Yom Kippur or Tisha B'Av. I still remember the smell of salmon and, sitting down at the dinner table, everyone actively debating, discussing politics and religion and relationships, and everyone getting very animated. To me it sounded like a long, continuous argument, and very different than dinners at my house. But it wasn't. It was an intellectual discussion, a deep debate and one of many I would experience at their table. Bill's parents, Bernie and Edith, had created an environment for openness and discussion that our group of friends adopted. We actively debated every topic under the sun, from Larry Bird versus Magic Johnson to American history to which stock we would pick if we had money to invest.

I am thankful to have had these relationships to nurture me on my journey. More were to come in college, and they endure to this day.

LESSONS LEARNED

- Let your childhood open your eyes to the world around you to imagine new possibilities.

- Cities can expand a child's view of the world and are vital to a state's social, economic and cultural health.

- Seek diversity to understand different perspectives and develop solutions that aren't one-dimensional.

Chapter 5

ANNAPOLIS: LEARNING TO LEAD

Looking back, it seems that I was meant to go to the U.S. Naval Academy, though at the time I wasn't so sure. The subject never came up in our house, but then it didn't have to. My father and his brother, Mike, had gone to Annapolis, as did my older brother, Paul. All of them studied electrical engineering, the most difficult program at the school. Eventually, somehow, I would, too.

Due to my father's commission in the U.S. Navy, and later his job at IBM, our family lived first in Groton, Connecticut, where his submarine was stationed, then in Potomac, Maryland. Then, after IBM transfers took us to upstate New York and to Reston, Virginia, we moved to Stamford, Connecticut, when I was 13. While living in Virginia and Maryland, the whole family would go to Naval Academy homecomings and football games and see the midshipmen in their smart uniforms—the Navy-blue dress with white and gold caps. For us, visiting Annapolis was a family tradition, but we didn't wear the Academy on our sleeves. It was just there, an unspoken presence, a part of the family.

All the same, in some ways I was an unlikely candidate for the Naval Academy. For one thing, early on in school I had a difficult time with math. I was not a very good memorizer, which made committing multiplication tables to memory difficult. I also had problems getting the concepts. (My mother, a grade-school math teacher, spent hours working with me until I outpaced her in trigonometry when I was a sophomore; by senior year, I was tutoring my friends in calculus.) For another thing, I was born with strabismus, a misalignment of the eyes commonly known as being cross-eyed or wall-eyed. I had the first surgery to try to correct the condition at nine months of age, followed by more surgeries at 11 months and at 5, 8 and 14 years of age. All the surgeries were performed by a surgeon named Dr. Marshall Parks.

As a result of my condition, I found reading hard, too. Compounding my difficulties was the awareness of my parents' accomplishments and the knowledge that my brothers were all smart, fast readers and quick learners. I had this pervasive sense of always feeling I was falling behind. And I was.

I remember coming home at the end of the first semester in ninth grade and handing my report card to my father. There, among other not-so-hot grades, was a "C" in chemistry. Normally, Dad would have raised his voice and asserted solutions to the obvious problem. But now, completely out of character, he suggested we go into the living room, a part of the house reserved for holidays and serious conversations. He studied my report card for what seemed an interminable amount of time. Finally, without raising his voice, he looked up and said, "You want your life to be a 'C'? Keep doing what you're doing." Then he threw the card back at me and walked out of the room. That was the first and last "C" I got in high school.

I knuckled down and worked hard. Going through moments of crisis and doubt, I learned to be calm under pressure, and reactive and resolute in making the right choices under fire. Success is about resilience—about "bounce-back-ability," if you will. That, at any rate, is how I programmed myself to respond to situations in which a lot was going on. Resilience is one of the most important attributes for someone in business or in public office, where the unexpected not only can happen but is certain to happen—and at any given moment.

Despite these challenges in my youth, I decided to apply to the Naval Academy. It wasn't as if I didn't have anything going for me: by senior year, my grades had improved significantly; as captain of my high-school soccer team, I'd demonstrated both athletic and leadership skills; and, as a budding entrepreneur, I'd managed a moderately successful landscaping business. Still, I wasn't all that sure I could get in.

First, there was the hurdle of the application process. As selective as Stanford or Harvard (I think applicants to the Academy have the same six or seven percent chance of acceptance), the Annapolis application process is more complicated and daunting. High-school seniors must first receive a nomination from the President of the United States, the Vice President or a U.S. congressman or senator. My nomination came from the late-U.S. Congressman Steward B. McKinney, whom I met during the interview process for Academy applicants. He was a larger-than-life presence, a man of the people, a fierce advocate for his constituents, and someone for whom to this day I have nothing but respect. He saw more potential in me than I think I did in myself at the time (his late-wife, Lucie McKinney, and her family have also had a great impact on me in so many ways over the years). Then, all of the nominations from around the country are sent to officials at the Academy, who determine the next year's freshman class by granting an appointment. While I was waiting for word of my appointment, the bad news came in the mail. I was disqualified on account of my vision: my eyes had failed the U.S. Navy's stringent regulations.

I was despondent and so were my parents. They decided to call Dr. Parks to see if he could help. What I didn't know until then was how well regarded he was, both inside and outside his field. I sat next to Mom as she called to tell him about my disqualification. "What?" I overheard Dr. Parks saying over the phone. "Well, he shouldn't have been because I wrote the regulations for the U.S. Navy, and he qualifies!" In a letter to the powers that were at the Academy, he effectively wrote, "Here are the regs. You can't reject him on account of his eyes. He may not be able to fly, but he can do all these other things." Dr. Parks' letter made the difference, and after an exhaustive eye inspection at West Point, of all places, the Naval Academy offered me an appointment to the Class of 1989, 30 years after my dad's graduating class.

I'd been recruited to play soccer at Annapolis, and I knew I wanted to study engineering, but what I wanted most of all was to learn to be a leader and to serve my country. Annapolis was in my blood and spirit—I was proud of the sacrifices my family members had made, and I was ready to do the same. The Navy would be a long, hard haul: four rigorous years of college followed by at least five years of active duty. But for me, the desire to be a part of something bigger than my own self-interests and to make a sacrifice for my country are what made me accept the Academy's appointment.

At the time, though, signing up may have seemed an odd choice. In the mid-'80s, America was still in the Cold War period and suffering from a kind of hangover from Vietnam. Young people weren't exactly rushing to join the military, which is probably why I underestimated the value of my choice.

At the end of senior year in high school, my parents and I were invited to attend the annual National Honor Society dinner. We dressed up for the event, as did the other students and their parents, which was held in the Stamford High School cafeteria. There must have been 150 people there that night. As kids' names were called and the colleges they'd been accepted to recited, applause went up for "so and so ... Duke," and "so and so ... Penn State" and so forth and so on. I was proud of what I'd accomplished, but I admit to having felt a little cowed by the achievements of some of my peers. Then I heard my name announced: "Steve Obsitnik ... the U.S. Naval Academy at Annapolis." The audience rose and gave me a standing ovation. I thought, 'Okay, this must be a big deal!' As it turned out, no one else from my class, and no one I knew from Stamford, was going to the Academy that year.

At that moment, I knew I was embarking on something unusual.

I now realize that from a young age people have looked to me to organize and lead. I'm not exactly sure why, except that I like to listen to others and channel their energy, and I've always been willing to stand up for causes when they need to be stood up for.

While my older brothers outperformed me in school, what the Academy apparently saw in me was someone who had compassion and leadership ability—someone with the kind of instincts, discipline and strong moral compass they could forge into a top leader. The mission of the Naval Academy is simply stated: "To prepare midshipmen morally, mentally and physically to be professional officers in the Naval Service."

On July 2, 1985, I entered the Academy on what we refer to as "I-Day," or Induction Day. In short order, I would learn a saying I still know by heart: "Annapolis is a great place to be from, not at."

Freshman year—or "plebe" year—is all about taking kids from high schools all across America and training them with a solid mix of rigor and discipline.

That re-tooling begins on I-Day in late June, when you report to school with nothing but a toothbrush and the clothes on your back. When my Dad reported for I-Day, he took a bus to Annapolis from Linden, New Jersey, because his parents couldn't afford to take a day off from work. I was luckier. My parents drove me down the day before. The next morning, we went over to the school, and I said goodbye to them at the gate.

Inside, any personal identity you think you have is wiped clean. Academy barbers shave your head, and upperclassmen take your clothes, which they stuff into a paper bag and replace with a uniform and plebe hat called a dixie cap, a white sailor's hat with a navy band, so that everyone looks exactly the same. From there, you're marched into Bancroft Hall, the students' dormitory. The instant you enter Bancroft, you hear the chatter and yelling from upperclassmen waiting for us to start our indoctrination.

The first upperclassman I bumped into was a guy named Mark Angel, who was a friend of my brother's. At the time, however, I didn't know who he was and he didn't know who I was. Basically, plebes must walk next to the wall—you can't just walk down the middle of the hallway— "square" all your corners and do what's called "chop-ping," which is like a slow jog with knees raised high. I was going up the outside of the staircase when Mark stopped me and had me "brace up," meaning I had to stand close to the wall and tuck in my chin. He proceeded to ask me a battery of questions I had no idea how to answer, keeping me there for 30 minutes or so and making me late for my next meeting. When I finally arrived, another upperclassman yelled, "Where were you?" In the Navy, there are only five answers, which you learn pretty quickly, to any question someone might ask you. They are:

"Yes, sir; No, sir; Aye aye, sir; I'll find out, sir; and No excuse, sir."

Two of these would come in handy many years later when my family and I were driving down the Henry Hudson Parkway into New York City one Sunday morning and were pulled over by a policeman. The officer got off his motorcycle—he was wearing big reflector sunglasses—came up alongside the driver's side and said, "Do you realize you were going 65 in a 55-mph zone?" I said, "No, I didn't, sir." As he was about to walk back to his motorcycle with my license and registration, he turned and said, "Is there anything else you'd like to say before I write up a ticket?" I heard myself say, "No excuse, sir," to which the surprised officer responded, "I can't give an honest man a ticket!" He handed me back my license and registration and let me go with a warning. I hadn't been trying to dodge a ticket, only relying instinctively on what I'd learned at the Academy.

By the end of that first day, you've gone from leaving your parents as a high-school senior to marching into Bancroft Hall as a plebe. My mother was in tears, but I could tell my dad was incredibly proud; I still remember the smile on his face. We said goodbye a final time, and I handed them the bag of my former clothing. All of a sudden, the bell rang—it must have been about six o'clock—and when it did, we left our parents and resumed the long journey toward becoming naval officers.

In addition to hair and civilian clothes, all privileges are taken away in plebe year. There were no smartphones at the time, but no refrigerators were allowed, no extra food, no CD-players or Sony Walkman radios. Nothing. Over time, you begin to earn back privileges and, in the process, see what you can do without. What you learn is that you can do without a lot. That is the whole philosophy. A lot of my education—through my parents, my grandparents and the military—centered on deferred gratification. Again, as my grandfather, Arthur Harden, would say, "There's a reason dessert is at the end of the meal, not at the beginning."

"The meal" involved rigorous academics, but it also involved learning how to fire weapons and how to box and wrestle—things most kids don't do in high school, at least not on purpose. You have to learn what it actually means to stand in place and take a punch, to be knocked down and get back up again and to wrestle with somebody who's 50 pounds heavier than you and find leverage points to beat him or at least hold your ground.

What's more, each year everyone has to jump from a ten-meter platform. This is a requirement; if you don't do it, you don't go on to the next grade. It's a simulation of jumping off a ship or an aircraft carrier if it were to catch on fire, but it's equally about facing a fear and being exposed to a crisis you may have to confront on your way to developing physically, mentally and morally.

One such experience happened during plebe year. I found myself in a college chemistry class and not doing very well. A few days after the mid-term exam, the professor pulled me and a classmate aside. "I don't know how this happened," he told us, "but your test results are exactly the same, and you've committed an honor violation." At a place like the Academy, violating the honor code immediately gets you expelled. The honor code is pretty straightforward: Midshipmen do not lie, cheat or steal. "I could easily refer this," the professor continued, "but I'm not going to. I just don't want this to happen again!"

I went to see my brother. His intelligence aside, Paul was a chronic renegade against authority. I thought he'd have some advice. "I don't know how this happened," I said. "I've never been accused of something like this!"

He said, "Well, if you didn't do anything wrong, then nothing's going to happen."

A month later, a week before Thanksgiving break, we were given another test. The following Monday when we returned to class, the professor had my classmate and me stay after while the rest of the class was dismissed. "Okay," he said in exasperation, "you guys did it again. Now this is going to the Honor Committee!"

I left the next day for Thanksgiving. It was a long drive with my brother back to Stamford. I hadn't been outside the gates of the Academy for five months, and what should have been an enjoyable ride home with Paul was painstaking. "I just got here, and I'm going to get kicked out," I told him. "And I didn't cheat!" And I hadn't. Paul assured me that the truth would come out, and all would be okay.

Returning to school—my head was still in a fog—I went back to the chemistry class for what I thought might be a final time. However, the professor pulled me immediately aside to say that my classmate, who'd sat behind me, had come forward and admitted he'd cheated off of my work. I thought to myself, 'How dumb is that! I'm not good enough at chemistry to be cheated on!' I'm not sure what happened to that kid, but I believe he eventually got expelled for another honor violation.

An unwritten part of the core curriculum at the Naval Academy is the lesson that one has to learn to follow before being able to lead. In freshman year, this lesson pervades every plebe's waking hours—and his sleeping hours, too. In effect, that first year is spent operating under pressure and trying to keep your nose above water.

For us, a typical day began with what is called "chow calls": Before a meal formation, we had to wake or call upperclassmen and yell at the top of our lungs, "Sir/Ma'am, you have ten minutes 'til morning formation. The uniform of the day is …, the officer of the watch is …, the midshipmen officer of the watch is …, the menu of the day is …," and so on. I still remember the face and sound of Midshipmen First Class Nick Connolly trying to distract me while I was doing this. At meals, upperclassmen would pepper us with questions about articles we'd read—the Laws of the Navy, profiles of Soviet ships, any type of detail to trip us up in a mental game that went on all year. What it all came down to was teaching us how to get through a stressful moment with clarity of thought and purpose.

But a greater challenge was about to present itself to me: electrical engineering. It was said to be the toughest major in a school known for being tough.

Many of the professors were Eastern European—one of my professors, Ralph Santoro, actually studied under Albert Einstein. Another professor, Anatol Sarkaty, had tossed Molotov cocktails at the Communist government of Hungary as a kid. About the only thing these professors didn't know was grading on a curve, and they had high expectations for me. Paul had gone through the program with a 3.8 average, which was extraordinary given that the Academy average at the time was around 2.7. When I showed up, they said, "Oh, we have another Obsitnik this year!," and my response was, "No, no. I'm here to balance the family average!"

Engineering allowed me to take a number of different disciplines and connect the dots to see how things work. At the same time, I was trying to build my own map of how the physical world functions. I didn't fully understand or appreciate what I was learning until I had to apply the fundamentals while on active duty on a submarine, but the Academy was a formidable place in which to begin to learn. I chose the path my brother had, knowing full well that my GPA would suffer, but I really wanted the skill set that comes with engineering. Besides, it was the hardest mountain for me to climb, and I always seek the highest mountain in front of me. That's how I'm programmed.

A professor who probably had the greatest impact on me at the Naval Academy was Professor Eberhart, who took notice of how hard I was working. He devised the initial Circuits class used to whittle down the 130 midshipmen who started off in electrical engineering; ultimately, only 19 graduated! Again, I felt I had to work harder than anyone else to stay even. On weekends, my friends would invite me to join them for a night out, and I'd have to turn them down because I had to study for a test or spend time in the lab. The test I was most worried about was the final for the first semester. I viewed it as the final for my entire career since it would determine who would be allowed to major in the program and who would be cut. I remember I had a 68 or 69 going into the exam—basically, a "D," a grade my father didn't know about. I went into Professor Eberhart's office and said, "I think I know the material, but I don't know how I'll do on the final. All I know is that I've worked as hard as I possibly could and am determined not to fail!"

Back home that summer, I went around saying, "Oh well, I tried but I'm getting out of electrical engineering." When my report card arrived a month or so later and I saw a "C"—actually, it was a "C-"—I was elated and said to my close friend, Bob Busby, now a successful patent attorney who was also vying to stay in the major, "We worked our butts off, and they noticed our potential. Next semester, we're going to visit each professor every day! They will just want to keep us around given our persistence." And they did. I learned that a good part of success is being committed to showing up every day, working hard and getting people engaged in your success.

And Professor Eberhart was engaged: he wanted me to show up next semester, and he wanted me to become an electrical engineer. It was the same with the other professors in the program. Professor Steve Burns ran the electrical engineering lab. He ingrained in us the need to bring theoretical knowledge into practice. In the end, this was the most challenging class—we had to pick a senior project and develop a product. Mine was a subwoofer simulator; it still works and is still in my attic. The Academy wanted young men and women who really wanted to study and learn the Principles of Engineering and commit themselves to them because they were training leaders to be engineers, not engineers who might eventually lead.

Plebe year ends with the whole class coming together in front of Herndon, a 21-foot-tall gray obelisk on campus named in honor of an Annapolis graduate and Navy captain who went down with his ship in 1857. At the top of Herndon, upperclassman tape a dixie cap then grease the entire monument. The goal is for plebes to somehow scale the obelisk, grab the dixie cap and replace it with a midshipman's visor hat. A thousand of us rushed the monument and had to figure out how to build a pyramid, people standing on people, to the top. To make the event more interesting, every 15 minutes the upperclassmen sounded a cannon, which shook the ground around the monument, threatening to topple us all. I don't know what the record is to complete the test, but it took us almost two hours. At the end, with the cap in our possession, we were totally covered in grease and sweat, but we were no longer plebes.

We had come through a rite of passage, a kind of ritual by fire. As iron isn't forged into steel until heat is applied, so too character isn't forged on its own. The whole idea of plebe year and of the Academy is to apply heat to people in order to forge them into leaders who serve in the Navy and protect and operate billion-dollar pieces of equipment—like a nuclear submarine in my case, or a nuclear power plant. At 22 or 23 or 24, you're in charge of service men and women, most of them older, who've been doing this all their lives. It is serious business; you're not only securing American citizens but you're in charge of people's lives and getting them back home safely.

Something else you're taught at the Naval Academy—and it's a big something—is that leadership includes taking the initiative without waiting for others to tell you what to do. You learn that when you encounter a problem, you don't turn away from it. You confront it, and you solve it. If this means going into a burning building, or any critical situation, you do it—even at the cost of limb or life. You don't pass the buck to someone else.

In choosing Annapolis, and submarine duty upon graduating, I learned to be a leader and to pursue an ideal and a goal. As Oma, my grandmother, had seen something in me, so had professors Eberhart, Santoro, Sarkaty and Burns. Success—in school, in serving your country, in business, in helping others—is all about creating connections with others and getting them to invest in your ideas and dreams. That's what leaders do, and it's what most people expect them to do.

LESSONS LEARNED

- Learn to follow: In order to be a leader, you first have to know how to follow others.

- Focus on the needs and desires of others: The perspective and empathy that comes from this allows you to better align a team's or institution's common interests.

- Discipline involves learning to do the right thing when no one is watching.

- Dedicate yourself to a project or a cause bigger than yourself.

Chapter 6

FORGING CHARACTER UNDER THE POLAR ICE CAP

L ike many college seniors, Naval Academy Midshipmen must choose their military career path in the fall of their senior year. The differences, of course, with few exceptions, were that our choices were confined to active military duty, requiring certain physical and mental, as well as academic, qualifications. The "job interview" and qualification process alone for each branch are long and rigorous. Interestingly, over time the civilian world has adopted many of these techniques.

After a Midshipman first-class, or senior, at Annapolis, chooses a military career path, he or she must then be accepted into one of five unrestricted career paths: The Marine Corps, including infantry and Marine Air; the Navy Seals; Naval aviation; surface ships; or nuclear submarines. The first two, I reasoned, didn't play to my strengths. Additionally, my history of eye problems would quickly have disqualified me from the third, Naval aviation. As for the choice between a surface ship and a submarine, duty aboard a sub just seemed a little more interesting and a bit more challenging to me. For one thing, service in the submarine force required another year or more of training after graduation in order to be trained as a nuclear engineer and learn the overall operation of a submarine.

I remember my parents taking us as kids up to New London to tour the USS *Nautilus*, the first nuclear submarine, and sitting on the jetties watching the black hulls of submarines leaving the Thames River as they headed out to sea. Additionally, the models of my father serving as a diesel submariner on the USS *Blenny* (SS-324) and my brother, Paul, serving on the nuclear-powered USS *Billfish* (SSN-676), were further incentives for a career in submarines. To be sure, military service was something that I was around as I grew up, and I had seen first-hand the thoroughness of the training and the many benefits my father and brother got from it, as well as what the country received for their service.

'Why not?' I thought. 'Everything else has been a challenge, why not take another one?' I knew sub duty would be rigorous—just *how* rigorous I would soon find out—but, as I reasoned, I'd just graduated with a degree in electrical engineering from a challenging and demanding institution, so I should be able to do this. The real question, though, and the one I would soon be asking myself, was, 'What in the world am I getting into?'

So, the interview process for the nuclear navy began. Admiral Hyman G. Rickover, the father of the Nuclear Navy, developed the now legendary, multi-stage career qualification process. This experience starts at Naval Reactors, a U.S. government office in Virginia just outside Washington, D.C. Admiral Rickover developed and ran the program for nearly three decades. As a first-class (a senior) at Annapolis, those chosen for the "Rickover treatment" spend two long days interviewing with nuclear scientists, officers and eventually the head of Naval Reactors to assess their capabilities and potential.

On day one, you're paired with a scientist and officers who spend the day with you, administering multiple tests that are videotaped and reviewed the following day by a panel of experts. One of the questions given to me by an intimidating nuclear scientist, I recall, went something like this: a car is being driven at a given speed with a pole attached to the roof and a tennis ball hanging from the pole. Under changing atmospheric conditions—this temperature, that degree of humidity, etc.—and going from 0 to 60 miles an hour in 20 seconds, at what angle would the ball be from the pole after five seconds of acceleration under these different conditions? This was designed to test problem-solving skills on the fly. (The interview style was very innovative at the time, and now many businesses have adopted some of the Nuclear Navy's techniques.) After two days of these interviews, if you were lucky, you reached "the final" interview with Admiral Bruce DeMars, who at the time ran Naval Reactors. This final interview with the admiral is legendary, and many have written about it. My father interviewed with Admiral Rickover himself and had to sit in a chair that had one leg sawed shorter than the others—to add a twist to the already-stressful process—in front the most powerful admiral in the Navy.

As I remember, I entered a room with a small table, two chairs and a desk lamp that seemed to hide the admiral's face. The interview was relatively short. "You didn't do too well on the test with the scientist," he said. "Why do you think that was?"

I knew the answer: they were impossibly difficult questions. But what I said was, "I wasn't prepared for the questions, sir, but it showed me that I need to vigorously prepare myself for all scenarios going forward. Never make assumptions, listen to those around you and then make your decision and be accountable. I'm 22 years old, and I'll learn from this." Admiral DeMars, seemingly unimpressed, asked a few more questions, then dismissed me with no sign of emotion. And I would learn from this interview, too, I'd only scratched the surface of the Rickover process.

After all the interviews, you're herded into a room with 100 or more friends and classmates with whom you've spent the past four years. Over the course of the next three hours, similar to the reality TV show "Survivor," names are called, and, one by one, you walk out of the room, passing your fellow classmates on the way. If your name is called, you're dismissed—meaning you won't be given a position in the nuclear Navy—and you have to exit the room past those 100 classmates who now know your outcome. The seemingly randomness of the names being called only adds to the anxiety. Sometimes they call out one or two names, and 15 minutes or more can pass before another name is called.

At the end of our stint in the room, an officer walked in and simply said, "You have been accepted into the Nuclear Navy."

That was in the fall of 1988. Following graduation in June 1989, I was assigned to temporary duty at the Pentagon, where for part of the time I worked with the Senate Naval Liaison, whose job it is to represent the Navy's interests with the U.S. Senate. That experience gave me an interesting perspective on public service. Walking the halls of Capitol Hill, corridors of policy, history and sacrifice, I realized how I was just one person in a long line of those who serve this country. Service and sacrifice are the reasons for being there.

From there it was off to Orlando, Florida, and Navy Nuclear Power School. It was, and I am sure remains, an incredible "manufacturing plant" of nuclear engineers. This program takes people with academic degrees in engineering, as well as people with liberal arts degrees, and puts them through a two-year graduate school–level course in nuclear engineering in just six months. To this day in my business career, I have never seen a system of training like the Navy's "Nuke" School program.

It began with a math and science test on day one before launching us into all aspects of reactor operation, including thermodynamics, electrical engineering principles, advanced mathematics and reactor physics. Based on the outcome of the tests, students were arranged by seat assignment in the classrooms. Those who scored highest were in the last row, and those who scored the lowest in the front row. Let's just say I wasn't in the last row. Before every test, a counselor sat down with us individually. Mine said something to the effect of, "Based on the history of all of the people who've been through this program, and based on your profile, we believe you'll get a …"—here he enumerated a rather modest grade— "… on the fluid dynamics test." I thought, 'Hmm. Well, I'm going to study and do better than that!' Sure enough, though, when the test was handed back, I saw that, lo and behold, I'd gotten the exact grade he'd predicted. And not just on that first test but on virtually *every* test! It was the most rigorous and academically stressful six months I've ever spent. There were only two days out of six months that I was not in that building working or studying. Since everything was classified, all work had to be done on site. Some classmates chose to drop out along the way, and some flunked out, including one guy who'd graduated in the top five percent of our class at the Naval Academy. I was shocked when I saw this happen. He was and is a good friend, and I always admired his intellect, quick mind and work ethic. Nuke School was obviously not for everyone.

At the end of these six months and before the final exam, the same counselor said to me, "Look, if you don't score higher than a 75 on this test, you're not going to move forward in the program." I scored 82 on the final, but the pressure and fun weren't over quite yet.

From Orlando, we got to choose between four nuclear-prototype facilities for practical reactor-operation training—basically a nuclear submarine's reactor on land. This schooling differed from the academic training we'd received in Orlando. Prototype training involved the operational aspects of the reactor, including overall training on all aspects of an engineering power plant used in a submarine. In other words, we were going to actually learn how to split atoms to generate steam to generate electricity and turn the propeller of a submarine.

I could have gone to training facilities in Idaho, upstate New York, South Carolina or Connecticut. I wanted to return home, so I chose Windsor, not too far from my hometown. On the first day we were told, "Here are books and manuals on the systems that convert reactor heat into propulsion. Get to work. These systems are what we use to operate a submarine, including hydraulics, reactor cooling, reactor control rods, electric steam turbines, propulsion turbines, diesel operation, steam valves, electrical breakers, mechanical propulsion, pumps, heat converters, reactor radiation and chemical testing procedures, necessary for maintaining proper pH, reactor coolant cleanliness and more." What's more, we were also told: "learn, trace, know every system in the plant—every electrical line, every pipe, every valve, everything—in six months." In order to do so, we would have to follow, or trace, each system to ensure we knew every detail and how these components were tied in together to achieve propulsion. This benchmarking process was rigorous, to say the least.

It was the first time in my life I found myself sitting in a functioning nuclear power plant. I was awed by the powerful yet practical design that allowed it to fit inside the hull of a submarine. I also found myself working alongside men from the fleet, some who'd been on subs for as long as ten and 20 years. They knew stuff I never dreamed of knowing. Adding to my awe was the potential danger in this environment. You're walking through a nuclear-reactor power plant on top of hundreds of pounds of uranium, seeing the output of one of man's most dangerous and powerful inventions, and you suddenly realize, 'this is *real*!'

Yet that training was invaluable. It fused for me academic knowledge, how things work, the ability to work alongside people who had more experience in their area than I did, and the necessity for clear communication and leadership. I had to find my own style for accomplishing the task at hand. The importance of having my own style would become very apparent once I was finally assigned to a sub and given a group of sailors to manage.

At the end of those six grueling months, we were given yet another practical operational test to qualify for running a nuclear plant in a submarine. You had to operate the nuclear plant for a six-hour shift while various drills were performed that challenged your ability to direct the staff and address challenges like steam-line ruptures, reactor scrams and catastrophic fires. I did pretty well at this test. It was five years of accumulated training that helped to prepare me for that moment.

After leaving Windsor, the final step of my training was three months at Naval Submarine School in Groton, Connecticut, where we learned how an actual sub really works in port or tactically at sea. This education includes interesting exercises such as "controlled" ascent from a submarine's emergency escape hatch, studying the operation and effects of nuclear weapons, and classes in catastrophic flooding. For the last exercise, you enter a simulated submarine compartment with piping and systems that have been riddled with holes and cracks. The operator turns on the water, which is close to freezing, and slowly the volume of incoming water is increased. Quickly, you and your team start to patch the cracks with pieces of rubber and rope and attempt to hammer in wood pegs to stop the flooding. The operator of the simulator continues to increase the volume and pressure of the water as it slowly rises from the deck and eventually reaches your chest. This simulates a situation that none of us ever wanted to face in reality. Added to this was training called "Mental Gymnastics": rapid-fire, complex math questions played over a cassette tape with only seconds to answer. It was kind of the math equivalent of "Name That Tune" or the modern-day "Beat Shazam." More fun was dive training where we operated in a submarine simulator that rocked about at all angles as we tried our best to keep from falling down and while practicing an emergency blow, or surfacing, of the submarine.

The fun just didn't stop!

Yet the reward finally came. I was 24 years old and received an assignment to report to the USS *Ray* (SSN 653), a Sturgeon-class nuclear sub home-ported in Charleston, South Carolina. The USS *Ray* (she was affectionately referred to by the crew as "The Mighty Ray") wasn't a new boat; it first launched 11 months before I was born. Not only that, but I was assigned to the same squadron my brother, Paul, had just been in. Basically, we tagged each other: as he was getting out of the submarine force, I was coming in, and I have to admit it felt a little odd being in the same place he'd lived for the past three years.

On my last evening before going to sea, I went for a final run on the beach on Sullivan's Island, a barrier island off Charleston. I always loved the ocean—I loved being on *top* of the ocean—and I thought, 'This is going to be the last time I'm going to run for a while and also the last time I'll be above the surface for possibly 120 days!'

Actually, I had no idea how long we'd be gone. When I reported to the ship, the COB, or Chief of the Boat, who was the senior enlisted man, told me a bit gruffly, "Just bring your toothbrush and whatever few personal items you want to have."

Green behind the ears, I asked, "How long will we be going to sea for?" I thought it a reasonable question. He looked at this newly arrived officer and said, "We can't tell you. We don't really know."

"That sounds like a long time."

He replied something along the lines of, "You can judge by the amount of food we're bringing on board. Welcome aboard, Sir!"

Generally speaking, he was right—life on a submarine is limited only by how much food can fit on board, though the reactor itself can operate for years. The first time I descended into the USS *Ray* through the main hatch, I saw that the low, narrow passageways, which were maybe six-feet-one-inch high by two-and-a-half-feet wide, were filled with canned food. You literally had to walk on cases of Hi-C and canned fruit, along with hundreds of oxygen candles, because space was at a premium. Literally, we would be eating our way home, and the further we went and the more we ate, the closer we would be getting down to the linoleum on the sub's floor and back to the U.S.

Meanwhile, the nine-man sleeping quarters I was assigned to actually slept 16 people. We called it "The Swamp." It held two officers and 14 enlisted crewmembers who had to "hot-rack" on seven of the bunks—while one was on watch, the other slept, then they'd switch. Having a bunk to myself was an obvious luxury, but it was far from plush, given the poor ventilation and the pervasive smell of diesel oil from the backup engine one deck below that permeated our books, clothes, hair and skin. Basically, when you returned to port, you threw out your books and clothes. The smell simply could not be washed out.

That first night aboard the USS *Ray*, I was awakened at 2:30 a.m. by the Captain, whom I'd only briefly met when I arrived a few days earlier.

"Wake up," he said. "We're going on a zone inspection."

A submarine is divided into compartments and zones, with zone inspections sometimes planned and sometimes spontaneous, as was this one. The Captain—I guess this is a diplomatic way of saying it—was especially "demanding." A zone inspection is done to find issues that may cause a problem in the operation of the submarine. At any rate, as we started walking toward the first zone, I was rubbing my eyes trying to wake up, and he was carrying a flashlight that had something like ten D-cell batteries and was so bright that if it were shined in my eyes it would have blinded me.

On the way, he said, "Tonight we are going on a zone inspection because your whole existence as an officer is to train yourself so that when you walk into a space you can immediately sense that something's not right. To do this, you must train and fine-tune your instincts and intuition to know what is normal and what is not. All of the training that you do comes down to a moment in time when you walk into an environment, and you just sense if something is right or wrong. A pump might not be going at the right revolutions per minute and put out a faint whine, the water-tight door maybe doesn't close correctly, a valve may be leaking, or the bilge may have an unusual amount of oil. Over time, having trained yourself, you will immediately know if there's a problem just by entering a space."

In the engineering room, where we would spend the next two and half hours, he said, "I'm going to shine my flashlight on something, and I'm not going to move it until you tell me what's wrong." He looked over my shoulder the entire time while we stared at one thing, sometimes for five or ten minutes. I was in a kind of meditative space in which everything was very quiet as I slowly become acclimated to the environment.

At last, for lack of any other clues, I said, "Um, there's a greasy fingerprint on the pump" and the Captain said, "That's right!" Off went his flashlight, and we moved on to another spot. We just walked around the entire engineering room that way: "The paint looks like it's about to peel!" "That's right!" But there were also a lot of things that I didn't pick up on, and he would say, "That's wrong, think harder, look harder!" They were very detailed things, from the size of a head of a pin to larger issues.

Touring the machine room on the lower level, I said, "You know, this pump doesn't sound quite right." I didn't really know what inspired the thought, but the Captain replied, "You know what? The impeller in there often breaks down and doesn't toss as much water as it should."

This was what was meant by training your instincts, so that, when walking around the sub, you would have an intuition about every piece of equipment in every space and how all the zones and pieces of equipment worked. Finally, hours later as dawn was no doubt breaking on the surface, the Captain shined his light on a sound-powered phone, and I said, "Uh, there's a smudge on the phone?" and he said, "You're done!"

During this process, the Captain looked up at me and said, "I am going to give you the most important leadership lesson I have learned."

I perked up after spending hours focused on details. "Leaders do one thing," he went on. "Leaders set the tone, tone defines the culture and culture is destiny."

It took me awhile to put these two lessons into perspective, however, because at the time I thought it was one of the craziest experiences I'd ever had. But the wisdom of really becoming so comfortable with yourself and your ability to understand the environment you're walking in—to know when something is right and when something is wrong—gave me a solid foundation of trusting my instincts and also of calling on others more expert than I when faced with something I didn't know. And the Captain's final lesson taught me how leaders can positively, or negatively, impact the destiny of an effort simply by the tone they set.

At any rate, that was the first night aboard the USS *Ray*. And, as with the 15 months of training leading up to this deployment, the night was far from over. Seemingly just a few minutes after my head hit the pillow in "The Swamp," I was up again and on high alert due to the presence, somewhere in the same sea as us, of a far-off Soviet sub.

Through all of this, perhaps, the greater education from serving at sea was in developing a leadership style that meshed with the crew, especially with those under my immediate command. A submarine is defined by specialties: sonar, engineering, torpedo, etc., and every junior officer is assigned one of these groups of men to oversee. I learned quickly that power doesn't come from the top down; your power is earned from showing people that you know what you're talking about, that you're actively listening, and that you have their interests in mind above your own. My approach to leadership was that I was there to learn from the crew in understanding how the sub worked. And as

Engineering Officer of the Watch charged with operating the nuclear power plant, I worked hard to do just that.

If you, as an officer, came on like Captain Queeg from *The Caine Mutiny*, the enlisted guys on board could quickly cut your legs out from under you. I knew, though, that my job wasn't about someone being an officer and others being enlisted: it was about being a team. One of the other junior officers on board tried the entitlement approach— "I'm an officer," he informed his crew. "I've earned this, and you're going to treat me as such" —and things didn't go so smoothly for him.

As with life outside the service, at sea, submerged for weeks or even months at a time, it really comes down to relationships and how people treat one another. On the USS *Ray*, that officer was "negatively impacted" by how he related to the enlisted men. Here is one graphic example.

Toilets on board empty into a sanitary tank, known as "sans tank," that, from time to time, is pressurized before waste is ejected overboard. Normally, the enlisted men conducting this task would put a sign on the toilets that reads, "Blowing Sans." The sign was put there to notify people the tank was pressurized. If you were to pull the side lever, it would force sanitary waste back at you with 30 pounds of force. Talk about a shower you never want to take! But, if the tank was pressurized, and one or more enlisted sailors didn't like an officer, they just might not put that sign up. Well, this young officer, a Lieutenant Junior Grade like me, was causing some problems for the crew. One evening when he went to use the toilet and saw no sign, he pulled the lever and, sure enough, he was showered with "waste."

In short, the crew tests you in the beginning. They are looking to see if you have operational knowledge as well as respect for their capabilities and, also importantly, a sense of humor and a sense of self.

The crew knows you've been to college. The crew knows you've been to nuclear training schools. The crew knows you're smart. What they don't know is what sort of person you are. What are your values, and how do you treat people? Naturally, they walk the line of respect but try to test you. If you show them respect, they back off and show you the same. I learned a lot about human dynamics while serving on board the Mighty Ray. In some sense, it was the best education I ever received.

You might imagine me being a little apprehensive coming from the Naval Academy with that "new officer" target on my back. But I developed my style of leadership to engage people person-to-person—to look someone in the eyes, explain my needs and understand his or hers. If I made a mistake, I owned up to it. I learned to laugh at myself, and to empathize and sympathize, but I also learned that it is important to expect responsibility and professionalism. It was an important lesson: Having expectations generates respect.

Aboard the sub, my approach to the largely-enlisted crew was essentially this: "Okay, I may be an officer, but I need you to help me to get qualified to run this sub, and you need to train me so I can better lead and work with you. Our lives and the safety of the submarine require that." I learned so much from the enlisted men on the *Ray*, many of whom were the smartest, most talented people I've ever worked with. I'm still in touch with some of them, and they went out into the world to be better engineers and to create some terrific businesses. On board, they taught me to lead them, and this is what I learned: leaders create and nurture followers, they don't force them. They become the kind of person others *want* to follow out of mutual respect.

At the same time, real-world responsibilities came with the job. To be 24 years old and handed the keys to a nuclear reactor worth a billion dollars was daunting. More daunting still, as well as humbling, was a year later becoming the Main Propulsion Assistant in charge of all the systems on board. Suddenly, in effect, I was responsible for the nuclear power plant of a U.S. submarine.

All of these achievements can be traced back to the mental, moral and physical preparedness I learned from my mother, father, brothers and instructors and classmates at the Naval Academy. It's about keeping mind, body, heart and soul in balance and honed so that you're always prepared for the leadership moment. When the moment comes, you're ready. It becomes the way you live your life. When you know that there are always bigger challenges to help people, you're preparing yourself to do that every single day.

LESSONS LEARNED

- Treat others with respect, regardless of their standing in the crew or community.

- Don't be a "sea lawyer," who makes excuses for his actions: Own up to your actions and take responsibility.

- Set a tone of what is possible: Tone creates culture and culture is destiny.

- Train your instincts to be ready to make decisions: If you need 100 percent confidence before making them, you'll probably miss the opportunities you are after.

Chapter 7

WHARTON: TRANSITIONING FROM THE MILITARY TO THE BUSINESS WORLD

T ransitions have their own timetables and agendas. They come at the cost of leaving where we are and what we know, and they're usually necessitated by a deep desire to grow and to thrive.

In 1994, after completing active duty in the U.S. Navy, I stopped home to visit my parents, who had relocated to Virginia from Connecticut, before driving up to Pennsylvania for the start of graduate school at The Wharton School at the University of Pennsylvania to pursue an MBA. This would begin my transition from the military to the world of business. I was excited to prepare for my future as an entrepreneur, and what better place to do that than at Wharton. I vividly remember the moment I learned that I was accepted.

Days earlier, I had been declined entry by a few other graduate schools and was a bit uncertain about my prospects for schools like Wharton. I was with my mom, and there was a rainstorm with sheets of water lashing the car as we drove up to our mailbox. I got out but didn't have an umbrella. The mailbox was stuffed with mail as often was the case. I have to admit, even today, our U.S. Postal Carrier, Nancy, gets frustrated with me for not checking the mail often enough.

Sorry about that, Nancy! Anyway, after a few attempts to extract the mail, a large white envelope fell to the ground face down. I picked it up and got back in the car, dropping the pile of mail on my mother's lap. As we drove up the driveway, she organized the mail and said, "Stop the car!" As my eyes met hers, she held up the envelope, showing me the Wharton insignia. "You know," she said confidently, "they don't send a thick package if you don't get in." We got inside, opened the envelope and read the first line of the welcoming letter: "We would like to extend you matriculation to The Wharton School," it read. I still remember the quality and length of the hug with my mother. I was going to Philadelphia!

Actually, before deciding to go to Wharton, I had started to look around at local business opportunities earlier that year when I'd realized I wanted to build upon my Navy foundation with rigorous business training.

In Charleston, South Carolina, where I'd been based, I was offered a job as a stockbroker with Edward Jones—one of thousands in that company—and another job as a chemical sales agent with Nalco. Both jobs were really interesting in their own way, but I soon decided that I needed to learn the basics of business as opposed to jumping into a job. I figured that business school would allow someone like me with no previous business experience to develop a perspective and navigate the business world a bit better.

Something else appealed to me about business school and Wharton. Similar to the Navy's nuclear-engineering program, Wharton had, and still has, one of the most rigorous and top MBA programs in the world. Also, when I was applying, the school had recently revamped its curriculum to focus on globalization, teamwork and diversity in addition to core finance, marketing and management skills. In fact, Wharton was ranked, for several years around that time, as the best business school because of these leaps in their curriculum. I do like to understand different people—how they think and feel, how they view the world and how their views can shape my own. I enjoyed a broad group of friends in high school and co-workers in the Navy, so I looked forward to broadening and deepening my perspectives on people, economies and the world at Wharton. And that, in fact, turned out to be the case.

The business school campus at Penn is a beautiful, park-like setting of tree-lined walkways and a green-lawned quad. More impressive than the place was the people. World-class athletes often talk about being on a "fast field" that makes them play at their best. We all get better when we are around people that push us to attain our goals. That applies to the academic, professional or non-profit fields we play on. I am not sure that I really internalized and understood that concept until I got to Wharton. As at any school, people defined the experience.

The professors at Wharton were impressive. The level on which they taught and inspired me was second to none. Professors like the legendary Jeremy Siegel were able to make sense of the U.S. economy and how financial markets behave. Another professor, Bob Inman, taught me about the micro and macro strategies of urban development and their importance to the growth of states and nations. One of the most memorable professors I had was Stuart Diamond, who taught negotiation and who has since played a role in the Middle East peace negotiations. Finally, Annie McKee was my leadership professor. Coming from the U.S. Navy, I had my fair share of leadership training, but she wove in the complexities of business ethics and situational awareness and how both are critical to success in business leadership. I am happy to call many of my former professors friends and mentors to this day.

Wharton students, meanwhile, came from so many countries and with so many varying backgrounds that it widened my world immediately. It felt like being on a fast field trying to keep up with people who pushed you based on their own experiences and, more importantly, their ideas and dreams. I am sure I added to the environment with my own viewpoints, but their presence definitely made me work and think harder. Although the academic program lasts only two years, Wharton gave me the chance to decompress from nine years in the military and to put into perspective what I had learned and what was possible going forward.

But let me tell you about my first day of class—a day that changed my life forever. Around noon on the first day of school, I grabbed a taste of local culture by buying a Philly cheesesteak at Sophie's food truck around the corner from Vance Hall, which I brought back to campus to have lunch and meet some of my classmates.

Two groups of students sat on opposite sides of the quad—eight or nine guys over here and six women sitting on the grass over there. I said to myself, "You know, I just got off a submarine with some 200 guys. I think I'll just plop down next to these women and say, 'hi.'"

The six women in the group were relaxed and very welcoming. I didn't make much of it—it was just having a conversation with new friends. Among them was a woman who had worked for a non-profit in Africa educating local people and providing access to birth control. Another new friend, Linda Chang, was an artist and marketer with a quick wit and keen sense of style. A few women were from Wall Street, all very smart and accomplished. And another woman, who had been part of the strategy team at Ernst & Young, turned out to be much more than a friend and an influence.

Her name was Suzanne Tager. She had flowing, dark-blond hair and was wearing a white button-down shirt with the sleeves rolled up, two buttons undone at the top and the shirt tails hanging out, jeans that had been cut into shorts and were a little tattered and sandals. Not long into the lunch, I said to her, "Do you want to go for a walk later and check out South Street?" And she said, "Sure."

One of the things that drew me to Suzanne was that she was so easy to be around. It just felt natural. Being with her was comfortable, it was conversation, it was dialogue. I'd never been in a relationship where it immediately felt like it was meant to be. I don't know about you, but it was the way it is when you talk to yourself sometimes, only there's someone there to listen. And I am happy to say we have been walking and talking together ever since that day in Philadelphia.

Suzanne and I took some classes together at Wharton, and I remember how she'd sit in the back of the room doing *The New York Times* crossword puzzles. When the professor would call out a question from the front of the room, she'd invariably look up, answer correctly, then go back to her puzzle. She blew me away with her intelligence, her independence, her organization and curiosity.

Inside our world at Wharton, which was like a bubble, things were very comfortable; but outside that bubble, life was more complicated. Suzanne is Jewish. I'm Catholic. At the time, and in the moment, this was a big hurdle for me, mostly because it was just different than how I was brought up. Everyone in my family had married within the Catholic Church with the exception of my maternal grandmother,

Annemarie m. My grandfather, Arthur, had a quiet, agnostic view, and my grandmother raised my mom and uncle, Art Harden, in Catholicism. My dad was a deacon in the church, too. So, you can imagine that becoming attached to someone of a different religious faith was not something that was a natural step for me, but, honestly, I don't think I ever thought religious sameness was a requirement for me and whomever I married. I wanted to find someone who had all the qualities that Suzanne had, and it just so happened she was Jewish.

The situation became easier for me when I met Suzanne's parents, Dr. Michael and Roberta Tager. Like her, they were and are very open-minded, welcoming and easy to be around. Michael was a surgeon at Norwalk Hospital for 42 years as a urologist. Even today, if I find myself in conversation with someone local who is 50 or older, there is a good chance he operated on them. His patients often say of him, "What a great guy. I love his sense of humor." I counter with, "But how did he do on the surgery?" The response—delivered with a blush, given his specialty—is "Great. Everything is still working!" My mother-in-law, Roberta (Bobbi) Tager, like my own mother, is amazing in her own right. She was also an elementary-school teacher early in her career. When still a young mother with three children, she was diagnosed with a serious illness and given a dire prognosis. Interestingly, she turned to holistic techniques, which changed her view of the world. The illness, thankfully, never took hold, and she became a trained holistic practitioner helping others for many years. Also, like my mom, Bobbi is one of my biggest fans. My favorite quote from her that I keep close to me, I think is ascribed to Wayne Dyer: "The problem isn't the problem; the attitude about the problem is the problem." I couldn't have picked better in-laws who, from day one, have been as accepting of me as of their own children. According to my friends, this is pretty unique, and for that I am so appreciative.

Just as Suzanne's parents treated me, my family liked Suzanne from the outset. Mom and Dad did have questions for me, though. The idea of a "mixed" relationship was as new for them as it was for me. They came of age during the 1950s and '60s. Since my grandparents had emigrated from Europe, no one in my family had married outside the Catholic religion. I spent a lot of time thinking about this. Suzanne and I had long discussions and talks about the bigger themes of raising kids. I read my fair share of books on the subject, but they all tended to have their own voice that was different from what was evolving inside of me. Most were too dogmatic, and they talked about Judaism and Catholicism in a vacuum, separated from each other, and the challenges that people *might* face in a mixed-faith relationship. I wanted to get married once, and I wanted our future children to have the strong family foundation that both I had and Suzanne had. Would we be able to handle the issue of religion? It took me over a year to figure this out. It was a process for me.

The biggest influence on me with regard to Suzanne—and virtually every one of my major life decisions since—was my friend, Manish Sabharwal. Manish had come to Wharton from Hyderabad, India. His global perspective and depth of understanding of topics, from philosophy to finance, challenges me like no other friend. We still banter and debate constantly. Good thing there's Skype and WeChat. Manish did and still does push me to expand my peripheral vision of the world. He would constantly say, "Expand your surface area of understanding." He expanded the breadth and depth of my reading. We attended as many on-campus speaker events as we could to learn from their experiences. I have found that a constant search to learn about new areas, ideas, disciplines and viewpoints gives a person perspective not only to understand a situation but to synthesize new solutions that previously might have been overlooked.

On one of our many walks and talks along the Schuylkill River, Manish cut to the essence of my quandary with a single question: "Why let man-made institutions keep you apart from the person you are obviously meant to be with?" This really set in motion a thought process of what was possible with Suzanne versus what I was reading in books. That is what good friends do—they question and challenge our own thoughts. With that breakthrough, the decision became clear in my mind.

The realization that I was meant to be with Suzanne was honestly more like a gentle sunrise than a Big Bang moment. I realized that, regardless of the constraints the world might put on us because of our religion, she was simply the only person I wanted to be with.

Suzanne, all the while, had been very clear about the issue. She said, "This is who I am. Don't compromise on who you are. We can, and will, work through any turns in the road ahead." If she was nervous at all, it was when she first visited my parents' house for Christmas when we were first dating. She had heard me talk about our traditional Slovak feasts but didn't really know what to expect. When she sat down at the dinner table, and my mother served 'Halupke,' Suzanne said, "That's just stuffed cabbage. I grew up eating this, too!" We quickly learned to focus on our similarities and priorities rather than on generalities and assumptions. The importance of finding common ground is a lesson that has served us both well in all aspects of life ever since. I am lucky that we have found a comfortable, workable relationship for ourselves and our daughters. It might not work for everyone, but we have not experienced many of the issues and tensions that those books I read in the early days predicted we would.

In spring of our second and final year at Wharton, a few months before we were to graduate, I knew that Suzanne would be going to Boston for a job and that I wanted to be there with her. I called up her parents and said, "Dr. Tager, I want to come up to Connecticut and take you to lunch tomorrow." I later found out that when he got off the phone, my future mother-in-law, Bobbi, said, "You know why he's calling! You know why he's calling!" Mike said, "Well, it could be one of two reasons. After all, I *am* a urologist!"

Well, Bobbi was right. I was coming to ask their permission to propose to Suzanne. I know that may seem a dated approach to many, but I respected her parents' opinion and wanted their support, especially given our religious difference. I wanted them to know that I was committed to Suzanne and to a relationship with them.

The next morning, I drove from Philadelphia in a monsoon-like rainstorm that lasted all day. I met my future father-in-law at Norwalk Hospital in the main lobby. He gave me a white lab jacket and said, "Let's go on rounds and meet some of my patients." We spent an hour or so visiting his patients. Remember, this was before HIPAA rules went into effect. We finally made our way to the hospital cafeteria. I stared at my pastrami sandwich as he picked up his open-faced tuna salad on toasted rye with a slice of tomato. How many times in our life is an important moment forever memorialized in what we are eating! I got to the awkward part of asking if I had his permission to marry Suzanne. With his quick wit, he said, "Well, you have to ask her." Then he quickly followed up, "Will you treat her well?" and I said, "Yes."

With that, he extended his hand, and I reciprocated. I am pretty sure I was more nervous in that moment than back at Naval Rectors in that interview with Admiral DeMars. Dr. Tager asked when I was going to ask Suzanne, and I said, "I have to leave some surprise for you and Mrs. Tager." With that, we continued on "our" rounds. From Norwalk, I drove into Manhattan to pick out a diamond from a dealer my Stamford friend, Bill Samers, had recommended. I'd never bought anything that expensive before in my life—I recall that the rule of thumb then was to spend two months' salary, but I *had* no salary and a dwindling savings account. After picking out a stone and having it put in a temporary setting, I drove back to Philadelphia completely stressed out.

That was in April, but I waited until graduation day, all the while keeping the most expensive purchase I'd ever made in my life in my apartment. Then, a few days before graduation, and unbeknownst to Suzanne, I'd gone to the Wharton office that produces some 750 diplomas each May and asked them to insert into her diploma a handwritten note congratulating her on graduating and attempting to capture my feelings for the future. At the graduation ceremony at Penn Convention Center, Suzanne went on stage to receive her diploma and returned to her seat. Once back at her chair, she opened her diploma to make sure they'd spelled her name correctly and found the message from me. She was stunned and all smiles.

Afterwards, we went outside, took some family photos, and the two of us started walking back to the quad where we'd met. At the base of the Ben Franklin statue near the Penn library, I bent down on one knee but stumbled and dropped the ring in the grass, where the diamond came loose from the temporary setting. Suzanne dropped down to help me find the stone, and after we laughed a bit, I asked, "Will you marry

*Arthur and Annemarie Harden,
my maternal grandparents, on
their wedding day.*

*Suzanna Obsitnik, my paternal grandmother,
back in Czechoslovakia before immigrating to
the U.S. in 1938.*

*The only picture I have ever
seen of Michael Obsitnik,
my paternal grandfather.*

Vince Obsitnik, my father, was born at home in this house in the former Czechoslovakia. The house still remains, but the roof was finally upgraded from thatched to tin. Courtesy: Vince Obsitnik

The plaque my maternal grandfather, Arthur Harden, was awarded for the best small business subcontractor in the U.S. and presented to him by President Ronald Reagan. Courtesy: American Products Company

The trip to Moscow that taught me about Communism and all that we have to preserve in the U.S. Pictured with my father, Vince, and younger brother, Jim.

Jim and I standing at the Berlin Wall.

My brothers at a young age:
Vince and Paul in the background
and Jim to my left.

The four Obsitnik boys
in our teenage years.

A recent picture of my parents,
Vince and Annemarie Obsitnik,
who provided me
with so much in life.

Standing with Paul Obsitnik in 1986 when he was a First Class and I was a Plebe (freshman).

My graduating class from the US Navy's Nuclear Power School.

First Class (senior year) picture at Annapolis.

Here I am leading 34th Company as their Company Commander in a formal parade.

Standing with my father at Naval Submarine School graduation in Groton, Connecticut.

Finally, a port call in Norway after a prolonged, Arctic Circle deployment.

Riding on top of the USS Ray's sail en route to port after completing a drug operation in the Central Atlantic.

The USS Ray in port after an extended deployment to the North Sea and Arctic Circle.

*Vance Hall at The Wharton School of Business and, to the right,
the quad where I met Suzanne Tager (my soon to be wife) on the first day of class.*

*The headquarters of SRI International (formerly the Stanford Research Institute)
in Menlo Park, California. Courtesy: SRI International*

An early picture of my "luxurious" office at Discern Communications in Menlo Park.
Courtesy: John Semion

Spanlink corporate photo taken just before the name was hoisted to the top of our new building.
Courtesy: Brett Shockley

Spanlink world headquarters in Minneapolis, Minnesota. Courtesy: Brett Shockley

A Brainstorming session with Quintel management as we created our initial business plan. Courtesy: John Semion

John Semion, my long-time CFO and friend, carrying our innovative antenna through the streets of Cheltenham, U.K.

Steve Bostwick and I at a Discern company picnic. Bostwick, USNA 1962, helped to create the Discern–Spanlink partnership. Courtesy: John Semion

Quintel's manufacturing facility as the team prepares to build product.
Courtesy: Lindsay Ager

This near-field, anechoic chamber is part of Quintel's advanced design and manufacturing facility.
Courtesy: Brent Irvine

While other cellular antennas were dangling after the hurricane season of 2017, the Quintel antennas came through undamaged. Courtesy: Joe Veni

Quintel antennas deployed in California. Courtesy: Joe Veni

Teaching my graduate-level course on entrepreneurship at
Sacred Heart University in Fairfield, Connecticut.

My family: Suzanne, Kayden, Kira and of course, Daisy.

R.V. One is my mobile campaign headquarters for the 2018 Connecticut Gubernatorial Campaign.

me?" All she said was, "Of course." To this day, I tease her that she never said "yes"!

Suzanne had known what she was going to do after graduation, so I had to figure out what my next step would be to join her in Boston after graduation. During the last year in school, I'd worked for the Wharton Small Business Development Center. The center was a partnership between the university and the U.S. Small Business Administration in Washington, D.C., where Wharton students teach classes, review the business plans of local entrepreneurs and help people with their business problems—in short, all the things someone has to do to start and grow a successful business. I worked there partly because I loved the idea of the place but also because the job came with a paycheck, which took some of the pressure off paying for my degree. As it turned out, this experience was invaluable because it gave me a practical, hands-on experience for what small businesses needed. I enjoyed working with people like the owner of a local supermarket on his need to expand his ethnic-food selection, and a local entrepreneur who wanted to bring tea to the world in the same way Starbucks did for coffee. It was rewarding work.

Like many other Wharton business-school grads, I applied to a few investment banks and consulting firms, but during the interviews my heart didn't exactly flutter. Leading into the last semester, however, I didn't have a job lined up. Suzanne was headed to Boston, and I knew my best "career" and "life" move was to follow her.

I had to move quickly to find a good fit in Boston. During the interview process, I got to know Michael Evanisko, the founder of Vertex Partners, a strategic-consulting firm initially focused on pharmaceuticals and healthcare. At our first meeting—again, here I am without a job or any real-world business experience—I said, "You're a consulting firm in the healthcare industry. The world will be changed by the convergence of communications and information technology. I believe you can expand your business in that direction."

I did know about these things—through my education in engineering and training on submarines—and had coded and written programs. I said, 'This is where the world is going," adding, "Look, Mike. I need to improve my business sense," (even after two years at Wharton, I was still not acclimated to the business world, and I knew I needed to get my land legs plus a little finishing!) "and you want to build your consulting firm." The job might not have been a perfect fit, but I needed to pay some bills, and I did see great value in learning the skills of a management consultant so I could more effectively frame business issues, develop pressure-tested ideas, communicate these ideas and, ultimately, convince folks that I could help their businesses grow.

With a mixture of confidence and bluster, I finished by saying, "I can build you a business plan to help move the company beyond pharmaceuticals and healthcare and into software and communication."

Mike and his team extended me an offer to join them. It was a big burden taken off my shoulders. Suzanne and I could now begin our transition to Boston. After Wharton, Vertex Partners turned out to be my finishing school, in the same way submarine training prepared me for the military. I learned how to think not just like a Navy submariner but like a business manager and entrepreneur. Vertex Partners helped shape my future in more ways than I could know, and the communications practice we started went on to be an important part of the business for years to come. However, in time I realized that consulting was not my true passion.

Along the way, I've come to appreciate and value the power of mentors, friends and relationships. First and foremost, they make up the very fabric of a life well lived. For me, they have also informed every business success I've had.

On a trip to San Francisco while I was still at Vertex, I reconnected with a friend, from Wharton, Michael Rose. He had told me about the company he was working with, which was led by an incredible founder. That person was Paul Cook, a Silicon Valley legend. Paul is a very successful scientist, entrepreneur, founder of Raychem Corporation and chairman of SRI International, formerly the Stanford Research Institute, previously part of Stanford University.

At my first meeting with Paul, he told me: "We're starting this company to deliver movies to the home."

I said, "You mean you're going pick them up at Blockbuster and drive them to somebody's home like a pizza?" At the time, remember, Blockbuster was a solid business and brand that was sold to Viacom for $8.4 billion in 1994.

"No. We're going to deliver them at four megabits per second over the cable system to a digital box, which doesn't exist yet, so people can just order a movie without leaving the house and watch it on their TVs."

The concept was called Diva. I realized what a big, bold idea this was and knew I wanted to be a part of the journey.

When I returned home from meeting with Paul Cook and his team in Silicon Valley, I brought with me a concept video they'd produced that showed what Diva would offer—vast selection, convenience, low cost, better user experiences—and I played it for Suzanne. When it was over, she saw my energy and the prospects for the future, and she simply said, "Looks like we're going to California!"

LESSONS LEARNED

- Transitions have their own timetables and agendas. They come at the cost of leaving where we are and what we know, and they're usually necessitated by a deep desire to grow and to thrive.

- Realize and value the power of mentors, friends and relationships. First and foremost, they make up the very fabric of a life well lived.

- World-class athletes often talk about being on a "fast field" that makes them play at their best. We all get better when we are around people who push us to attain our goals.

Chapter 8

LEARNING TO INNOVATE IN THE SILICON VALLEY

For someone who has always been curious about how technology and science can come together to solve people's problems, going to Silicon Valley and having open access to research labs filled with scientists and software developers was like being a kid in a candy store. That period marked the beginning of my business career, being trained—and training myself—to use technology to innovate, overcome challenges and address big problems with real solutions.

My Silicon Valley experience began when I walked onto the campus of SRI International, formerly the Stanford Research Institute, a nonprofit research center acknowledged by many as the epicenter of Silicon Valley and in close proximity to Stanford University. A $500-million institute, SRI develops new technologies for governments, nonprofits and corporations, and is simply one of the greatest R&D organizations in the world. Over the years, SRI technologists have created products that include airplane stealth technology, ultrasound, speech recognition and the da Vinci Surgical System.

SRI was also home to the venture that Paul Cook created with a vision to deliver movies to homes over cable. It was a big, bold, audacious vision and something I knew the future would embrace. It was called Diva Systems and was housed on the campus of SRI in 1940s

Quonset huts that had served as hospital units for veterans coming back from WWII and the Korean War. I wouldn't have wanted to work in a gleaming, high-rise, corporate headquarters; I liked being in a Quonset hut because it felt like a workshop. At Diva, I had free access to facilities on the SRI campus. I would walk through the artificial intelligence (AI) lab or the chemistry lab or the education lab, getting to know the people working there and understanding what they were doing. Over time, I found myself coming back to the AI team.

I created strong relationships with three of the people I met there—I called them "The Three Amigos"—who to this day serve as friends and mentors. David Israel was the Director of Natural Language. An out-of-the-box thinker, he has instructed some of the biggest AI successes for the U.S. government; a word he commonly uses— "groovy" —provides insight into his makeup. Jim Arnold, Director of Software Development and a soft-spoken Wisconsinite, taught me how to break down customer problems and give them back software solutions. Michael Summers, a street-smart guy from Chicago and Director of Ventures and Licensing, took me under his wing to teach me how to create business models and structure deals.

In those days, I spent a lot of time looking into a project (later called Siri) that AI innovator Adam Cheyer led. Its potential was great, eventually finding its way to the Apple iPhone, but the timing was too early in 1999. These conversations and early experiences came to define me as an entrepreneur and a leader. I'm drawn to more than one area or experience—I like being able to synthesize across many disciplines and peoples' experiences to help chart a course for a company or an industry. SRI gave me that perspective to look beyond the obvious and ask the important question: "Why not?"

My first job was working as a product manager at Diva. As it turned out, the role was similar to being a junior officer on a nuclear submarine. Product managers have to have solid, general-management skills, technical competency, an outward view of the world, the ability to listen to customers, and the capability to mobilize people to accomplish ambitious goals on tight time schedules and shoestring budgets.

Diva did well in the early days, going from a concept to the largest deployment of video-on-demand in North America and the United Kingdom. As Michael Rose, Vice President of Corporate Development, recalls, "As a team, Diva created the foundation for the industry for what was possible with interactive TV."

We created and delivered on some of the earliest concepts of video-on-demand that today have become commonplace. In addition to technologists, Diva had a great content-licensing team. In particular, the quick-witted Mike Davis from Thousand Oaks, CA, taught me how to talk technology to Hollywood. Creating technology is one thing, but to get world-class companies to accept it is another. Together, Diva created the first "streaming" offerings of on-demand TV for ESPN, Disney, Showtime and HBO. We were also the first company to demonstrate "time-shifted TV"—the cloud-based DVR we all live with today. Back in 2000, it was not legally possible to deploy this capability in "the cloud" due to licensing rights. I thought we could be more aggressive in bringing this capability to market, but as a company Diva wasn't ready to take that step beyond its core product.

For 1999, we were ahead of the times in many ways. We had to build out virtually the entire ecosystem, from digitizing content to billing systems and even digital set-top boxes. That was a lot for any company, let alone a young, startup. We also found ourselves dancing between two industry forces: cable operators and content providers. As they saw the impact and threat to their own business models, they started to act in more protectionist ways. Eventually, the HBOs of the world started saying, "Hey, why are we licensing our content to these guys?," and the cable operators were saying, "Hey, why are we giving them a percentage of our revenues?" As technology started to commoditize, new entrants came into the market with their own solutions to overcome some of the barriers.

A few years later, a startup called Netflix began shipping movies to homes—the same concept as Diva but via the U.S. Postal Service instead of a cable network. They had the right business model—go direct to the consumer. Some 15 years later, they and others succeeded in fulfilling our vision of delivering video and on-demand content to customers. Needless to say, I learned a lot.

Yet, all experience is instructive, especially the challenging times in our lives. My time at Diva yielded three valuable lessons and takeaways:

One, timing is critical to any project: As Curt Carlson, former CEO of SRI, famously says, "Developing a new business is not about failing fast to know if your product is viable, but learning how to succeed fast, which is critical." Ideas like "lean startups" and agile development aid in this process.

Two, similar to what I experienced in the Navy and at Wharton, put yourself on a "fast field": World-class athletes talk about how being on a fast field makes them better. Diva and Silicon Valley gave me another opportunity to be on a fast field. Surround yourself with the best, and you will be better and so will your product.

And three, to create new industries that bring more people into the workforce, we must create a culture that, from the earliest stages, allows people to experiment and develop bold, new ideas. We may not always get it right, but innovation is what changes the world.

After earning an MBA from Wharton, I knew that I wanted to start my own business one day. Part of this drive, no doubt, came from sitting in my grandfather's machine shop, listening to him talk about the company he'd created and how American Products parts found their way into the space shuttle and IBM disk drives. That was cool to me. But another part sprang from my desire to create a venture by building my own team of talented people.

One day while still at Diva, as I was talking with Michael Summers, I said to him, "Why don't we work together to spin out a new company?" After Michael and I white-boarded some concepts, and after a lot of deliberation with Suzanne who challenged my thinking, I went to see Paul Cook, who was chairman of both Diva and SRI, to get his perspective and, hopefully, his permission to leave Diva to start a business. It was a hard conversation because Paul had taken a chance on me and given me a lot of responsibility. I explained about the spin-out opportunity and my desire to create a business and step out on a limb as a CEO for the first time.

"You know," Paul said, "there are a lot of people who I wouldn't encourage, but I know you have the leadership skills, vision and temperament to do this. I am supportive of you taking the leap. Let me know what I can do to help." I felt a big burden lifted when I heard those words. I work hard to preserve relationships, and this remains an important one. With Paul's support and confidence, I was off to work on my new adventure.

Several years earlier, I had worked on a project for the U.S.

government at the AI lab at SRI that contributed to something called the FBI Carnivore Project, later renamed DCS1000. With the growth of email, the FBI needed to implement a system to monitor emails and electronic communications; their goal was to search emails for words and phrases that might indicate illegal and possibly terrorist activity. The project, like many others, had come through DARPA, the Department of Advanced Research Project Agency, which was part of the U.S. Department of Defense. DARPA has a mandate to develop emerging technologies for military use, and many commercial benefits have come from their work, including the development of the Internet. DARPA principally acts as an intermediary between the government and places like Stanford University, SRI and MIT, with the capability to solve big problems. Once a problem is solved and a solution developed, the U.S. government uses it for its own purposes, while granting R&D organizations like SRI the commercial rights and the freedom to take the innovation forward. One commercial product that came out of the process was the computer mouse, hatched in the SRI office of Doug Engelbart, a pioneering innovator. It just happens that Doug's office was five doors down from mine.

The interesting thing about my association with SRI is that I was never an employee—I was there because of relationships, which may be the most important factor in business success and certainly the most important in my evolution as a leader in business and in public life. Without close, genuine relationships, there can be no trust, no true inspiration, no collaboration. I have learned that building trust is the most critical element to make anything in life grow. Personal relationships with your spouse and kids; comfort in dealing with a business, knowing you can return a faulty product; confidence in your elected leaders—all these aspects of life demand trust.

By the late '90s, SRI was attempting to start up and spin out two to three companies a year. From the AI lab, it had successfully spun out Nuance Communications, the first company to deliver commercially viable speech-recognition tools. Soft-spoken Jim Arnold's experience in that venture helped us in our new venture.

Meanwhile, the AI lab and I began the formation of Discern Communications. I was employee number one. Curt Carlson, the CEO of SRI at the time, showed great confidence in me and taught me what it takes to make a business successful: vision, persistence and a lot of grit. As Curt remembers, "Steve's military background and Paul Cook's endorsement were big factors for me, but I saw someone who could withstand a lot of pressure and adversity. You need to do that to run a successful technology company." With Discern, it was less a question of the quality of the software code and more about applying the software to an important problem where we could deliver a compelling value proposition. Added to that was convincing employees to join our mission in a very competitive labor market, customers to try our product and investors to give us a chance to make it all a reality.

As CEO of Discern, my job was to create the vision and business plan while defining the product, raising capital and hiring talent to form a compelling offering to the outside world. But this time around it wasn't only about timing, it was about finding the right problem to solve. At first, Discern was focused on Internet search capabilities. Google was just starting up at this point—around 2000—but there was already Alta Vista as well as many other search engines. The tech bubble burst just as we were starting, followed by the stock-market crash. Overnight, it became hard to raise money, and we were unsure how to apply the code base we had developed.

What did we do? The only thing *to* do: I brought my team together for a two-week brainstorming and market-analysis session. We looked at industry trends and visualized where we needed to go. An article caught my eye, citing that there were more call-center agents in America than there were teachers. Even today, there are over 2.2 million workers employed in over 6,800 call centers in the U.S. I thought, 'Now that's really interesting.' Then I read that for every second American Airlines could shave off time spent on the phone with a customer, it could save the company $1 million a year. My next thought was, 'There are a lot of people who could use better customer service, too. How does an agent go through thousands of documents to find answers to customers' questions?' So, I sat down with Curt Carlson and Hal Kruth, who was the Vice President of Ventures and Licensing for SRI at the time, and gave them a thoughtful, detailed presentation on the customer-care market size, segmentation, trends—everything—along with a big stack of data, and Hal Kruth stopped me in my tracks. He pushed all of my data to the side of the table and some of the charts fell to the ground.

"Is there something wrong?" I asked.

Hal looked at me and said, "People don't want to know about numbers, Steve. People want to know how you're going to change their lives." And he added, "This is technology, we're engineers, and it's easy to fall into that trap, but we're not here to make numbers better, we're here to bring value to people's lives. Don't *ever* forget that. Come back and tell me how you will achieve that."

I closed my laptop, gathered my data and left one of the most impactful meetings, and with one of the most important life lessons,

I've ever had. I had a lot of work to do to strength Discern's value proposition to customers. Ultimately, it is about how people feel about your product and if you meet a real customer need.

Since then, in every project I've worked on, when dealing with others, I'm Hal's disciple and messenger in saying, "Look, it's not about the inside, it's about the outcomes. How do you make people's lives better, how do you keep them healthier, how do you improve their quality of life? You can't lose sight of the forest for the trees—or the people who live in the forest!" These are lessons that I always try to keep in the forefront of my mind when dealing with people and the projects and policies that affect them.

Important in our process to find a market for Discern was the value-creation tool developed at SRI—an innovation framework that is straightforward and applies, I believe, to states as well as to companies. Curt Carlson made it his personal mission to ingrain this framework into everyone's thought process. He would say, "We are building billion-dollar companies here. That takes hard work constantly refining a value proposition to reach that goal." He called it the "NABC framework," which breaks down into four basic questions to answer.

N is for Need—what is the true market need a customer has? It must be a clearly defined need; an idea is only an idea.

A is for Approach—what is your unique approach to addressing the need?

B is for Benefit—what is the qualitative and quantitative benefit for the cost that your unique approach brings to that customer need?

C is for Competition—how do you differentiate yourself from the competition in the market being explored? —because there is always competition.

After reorienting our business plan around customer care, we rapidly got to work building a suite of software tools focused on customer, agent and supervisor self-help. Our customers ranged from Dell to BusinessWire. The software was customer-friendly and responded efficiently to natural-language queries. For example, if someone asked, "Who acquired Fleet Bank, and how much did they pay for it?" Discern would respond with a specific answer, as opposed to thousands of links. Customer service representatives would use it in a similar way to search hundreds of databases, manuals and technical documents to come up with an answer while on the phone with customers, both shortening the response time and improving the customer experience.

This was happening in 2000, a time when companies had begun off-shoring customer-care services overseas. Our software allowed us to help our customers keep more jobs in America by making customer-care interactions more efficient and providing customers a better experience.

Getting the idea developed, the product built and customers buying it, however, took time, and we struggled.

Discern was operating on a tight budget. We were always able to pay our employees on time, but there were times when I and my senior leadership team had to forgo our salaries. At times, we felt like wounded tigers trying to stay alive. The odds were against us, for sure. In a start-up company, money is oxygen, and when investors stop funding a venture, the oxygen is gone and teams disband. But my team, which ranged in age from a 22-year-old, college-grad techie to a 45-year-old product manager, had so much heart and soul that nothing could stop us. We simply knew how to stretch a buck and drive value for our customers.

What I found from this experience is that in most projects, if you limit the amount of money people have to spend, teams make better, more innovative decisions because they have to figure out how best to use scarce resources and maximize opportunities. In short, budget constraints often force people to make decisions, good or bad. As a team, the members can then rapidly adjust their strategy. By 2002, we started to hit our stride.

That was one lesson in the value of perseverance, without which most people never realize their dreams. But an even more important lesson came out of the first significant deal I did at Discern.

Word reached us that the CEO of a prospective customer was interested in our product but told his people, "I'm not going to sign a deal with an upstart company until I meet the CEO. Have him come see me."

'Fair enough,' I thought. I flew to Dallas and sat in the reception area outside the CEO's office for over an hour before he finally emerged and said, "I have to fly to Chicago. You can meet me there if you want."

"But sir," I said. "I just need a few minutes with you."

"I don't have a few minutes," he said, and with that he headed for his corporate jet and the flight to Illinois. I had no choice but to follow.

At the Chicago hotel where he was staying, he told me, "I have a customer dinner and don't have time to talk now. You can meet me in the lobby tomorrow morning."

Waiting for him in the lobby the next morning, he said, in passing, "You know what? I've been diverted to Washington. Meet me there."

So, I flew to Washington, where I finally met him. "Oh, you!," he said, as if surprised to me.

"Yes, sir!"

"Well, now I have to go to London."

At this point—the third leg of a journey that appeared to have no actual destination—I felt like I was on a wild-goose chase.

I said, "Excuse me, sir, but I can't *afford* to go to London. I can't afford to go anywhere else. I know that you want to talk to me about this deal, so, please, just tell me what questions I can answer for you about Discern."

And he said, "You've already answered it by following me around. I see that you want this deal a lot, and I know that if something goes wrong, you'll be there. I will have my team execute the contract."

That deal was what the business needed, what my team needed. That deal gave us stability and me the unshakeable belief in people and relationships.

What my time in Silicon Valley did for me was two-fold. First, it gave me a deep understanding of what vibrant ecosystems feel like and that these can be formed in other parts of our country. Second, it personally forged all of the leadership skills, team-building, entrepreneurial drive and industry experience together in a way that allowed me to compete successfully in the market. Looking back, Silicon Valley helped to set the stage not only for more opportunities for me, but also for the knowledge that once the right environment and ecosystems are created, anything is possible.

LESSONS LEARNED

- Begin with what is impossible and make it possible.

- Don't try to force a plant from a seed: ideas take time. You have to commit to the idea and dance with it as it changes and grows.

- There are no golden rules in entrepreneurship, no perfect idea or opportunity, and no perfect time to start. You just have to start going down the path.

- De-myth the idea of the individual hero: Entrepreneurship and business are team sports, and strong teams are more about the chemistry of the people as a whole than about the biology of any one person.

Chapter 9

GROWING A BUSINESS IN A
COMPLEX WORLD

While still in Silicon Valley, relationships based on shared experiences and values led to yet another unforeseen opportunity and new adventure.

An Annapolis alumnus introduced me to a 1962 graduate named Steve Bostwick. "You're both Naval Academy graduates," the alumnus said. "You're both good people and doing things in the same industry, and you should get to know each other."

Steve, who had graduated from the Academy the same year as my Uncle Mike had, was a straight-talking Kansan with a Midwestern accent who was based in Minnesota. He and I met a few times and talked about the company he worked for called Spanlink Communications, at the time a consolidated subsidiary of Cisco Systems that was part of its Voice-Over IP (VoIP) customer-care solutions. As head of sales at Spanlink, Steve saw an opportunity to sell Discern's products through Spanlink's sales force. After a few meetings, he said to me, "How can we work together?"

He then introduced me to his boss, Brett Shockley, Spanlink's founder and CEO, and an out-of-the-box thinker, true industry visionary and interesting individual, to say the least. At 16, I believe, he held the Guinness World Record for riding the tallest unicycle while juggling! Like me, Brett enjoyed going into labs—he'd actually worked at Bell Labs. He had started Spanlink to focus on what was then called Computer Telephony Integration, bringing software solutions to call centers. There was a steady and constant evolution in this area, and Brett and his company were as innovative and creative as we were. I often think of a quote from Marcel Proust, the French novelist, about ideas: "The real voyage of discovery consists not in seeing new landscapes but in having new eyes." This describes Brett well. He has a unique ability to look at a problem or situation and see a fresh perspective or opportunity.

I saw this new relationship with Spanlink as a way for my team to expand the breadth and size of our opportunity, while adding a new capability to expand Discern's market reach as well.

I also realized that companies were beginning to switch, and rapidly, from analog circuit-switch dial tone to voice-over IP—a big-tech transformation for businesses—and VoIP systems were being rolled out in call centers across the U.S. VoIP systems offered great advantages to both small and large businesses. With them, companies could significantly reduce their costs, operate more flexibly and improve their business processes to be more efficient. For example, a small business could more easily add new users and have them located anywhere without complex hardware changes. Likewise, a larger customer like Wells Fargo could treat its hundreds of branch offices like one integrated, virtual network. This meant that the company didn't have to have every type of banking expert in every branch location. Customers in Boston calling their local Wells Fargo office could be routed seamlessly to an expert who, for instance, happened to be at a branch in Charlotte, North Carolina, and would be able to answer customers' questions on the spot.

To make this all happen required more than simply changing a phone signal from analog to digital. It involved mapping a business' processes and overlaying the new technologies. Customers had to think differently about their own business, which made them more creative. We incorporated a number of technologies, bringing together things like speech recognition, text-to-speech, speech-to-text, advanced call-routing applications and deep database integrations. The result, when done right, not only got a customer to the right person to answer his or her question, but it delivered the right information and popped it on the agent's or customer's screen almost immediately. These system deployments were complicated and required capabilities in this new world of VoIP that Discern and Spanlink were uniquely able to address.

The timing eventually resulted in the acquisition of Discern by Spanlink. We simply saw that we could be stronger and faster together, with us bringing our unique intellectual property and product to Spanlink to enhance their and Cisco's contact center offering. Spanlink and Cisco brought industry experience, their own products and a much larger sales force. As I mentioned, Spanlink was headquartered in Minneapolis, and I took on the role of President, working closely with Brett Shockley. Since Suzanne and I were still living in San Francisco at the time, I would leave there on Sunday night or Monday morning and come back home on Friday night. I spent the next year commuting weekly between Silicon Valley and the Twin Cities.

In addition to experiencing a bit of culture shock in Minnesota, I also experienced climate shock. The first time I went to Minneapolis was in the winter. I'd left my laptop out in the car for a couple of hours and when I finally brought it back into the hotel and tried turning it on, it wouldn't start. It took popping out the battery and warming it under my arm for a few minutes before putting it back in to get it to start.

If it was a sacrifice for me to commute halfway across the country every week, there were also sacrifices made by my family. My brothers lived in California, our friends were close by and Suzanne was doing well in her career. It was during this time that our eldest daughter, Kayden, was born. Added to the stress, Kayden's birth had its complications which resulted in an immediate surgery and an extended stay in the neonatal intensive care. The burden of my travel, and Suzanne's work and caring for Kayden, started to mount. Honestly, the back and forth was less than optimal for the business as well.

Then, after months of living out of a suitcase and having many conversations with Suzanne, I came home from one of my week-long trips and opened the door to find Suzanne standing there holding Kayden. Both had on flannel shirts and trapper hats with earflaps. "We're in. We should all go to Minnesota," Suzanne said.

With that, we planned a trip to Minneapolis to see what it would be like to live there with Kayden, who was eight months old at the time, and to see if this was what we really wanted. It was on that trip that we said, "If we're ever going to make this move, we should do it when our kids are young, before they established roots."

In her wisdom, Suzanne was clear in her advice that it was best for Spanlink to have a leader who was on site and not constantly flying in and out as a business nomad. In a connected, digital world, it is easy for people to become hidden from one another or to bring people together only once a week by plane or train. This can work, but I have found it can often lead to miscommunication and lack of alignment. Business is about people and relationships. These interactions strengthen when people are able to come together and spend time together solving problems.

With the move, Suzanne decided to put her career as a management consultant on hold. Behind this was her belief, as she had said early on in our relationship, that life is about adventures and you have to commit to opportunities. She's always been good about that, saying, "If you find something worthwhile, you can't straddle the line."

Whenever I settle into a leadership role, as I did during our time in Minnesota, I am usually very aware of the prevailing culture and how best to motivate change and allow people to move beyond hurdles. During my first year there, an important piece of software that was a part of Cisco's product had to be shipped on time, but we found ourselves behind schedule and with a large economic burden if we didn't deliver. Pulling the entire engineering team together, I said, "We're two weeks away from the ship date to Cisco. If by the end of this week, we haven't figured out the bugs in this software and have a clear path to deliver it, we will all have to cancel our weekend plans to get the job done."

Almost in unison, everyone's heads came up, their eyes got bigger as they met mine. Everyone was staring at me. After a long silence, one relatively junior engineer in the front row raised his hand and said, "Excuse me, Steve, but you do know what this weekend is, don't you?"

"I have no idea what weekend this is," I said. "It's a weekend."

"Well, it's the opening of deer-hunting season!"

And I said, "Well, now you know what you have to accomplish before then," and I briskly left the room.

Deer-hunting season in Minnesota, I learned, is almost a religious holiday, and I nearly had a mutiny on my hands. On the other hand, this call to action was just what was needed for the mission to be accomplished—and it was. We fixed the bugs and shipped the software, and I was not run out of town!

All in all, the combination of Spanlink and Discern, even with its various bumps at times, progressed well. One reason the combination worked was because Brett and I worked together well in terms of our roles and how we complemented each other. We both are strong technologists, both straight-shooters, and we both create good relationships around trust. What's more, we were in this for the right reason—to build a bigger business together—and we'd made sure that our interests were aligned. I was committed to growing his business, and he saw the value of what Discern was bringing to Spanlink. We both had solid operational discipline and visionary thinking. Brett, in particular, taught me a lot about higher-level relationship management. And we both realized, I think, that we could learn something from one another.

All the while, what I liked doing was making sure that the business was set for growth, and that was about doing four things well up front to drive a clear vision and alignment for us across the business. The four steps we applied were:

Build a situational fact-base: Develop a clear reality of our situation in order to set up decision making and ask critical questions: What are the industry trends and market factors? How are these helping or impeding us? What are our assets, both internal and external, to the business? Finally, being as clear-minded as possible, weigh our challenges, opportunities and threats.

Create a unified strategy: Determine and develop our strategy in terms of where our combined organization can go forward, specifically in regard to our products and services and the distribution channels, the size of the workforce that we can attain and our hiring plan.

Determine whether the strategy fits the reality: Overlay on our strategy the answers to these key questions: What is our need? Does our approach address it? What is the benefit we bring? What is the competitive set and reaction? (This is just what we did back with SRI and Discern in reference to the NABC innovation model.)

Monitor and measure execution of progress by asking: What is our plan to execute and how will it be communicated? Ensure we can measure performance—put the "electrodes" on the business, in other words, and at the right level, and are actually going to lead the organization in the right direction to the desired outcomes.

In addition, I created metrics across four areas that allowed us to hold business reviews in order to track our success and see if we were achieving our goals. The areas that we were going to monitor included financial metrics, customer metrics, employee metrics and operational metrics. Those were my "electrodes" to measure the business so that I could tell every week, as well as quarterly, that we were achieving our mission together.

One way I personally measure my own success and derive personal value is to identify talent that can succeed after me. None of us is permanent in any role, and we have to leave an institution stronger than before us with people who, hopefully, can do an even better job. At Spanlink, I recognized talent in abundance in two young people. The first, Melanie Meier, was an internal accountant when I arrived. It was clear that her work ethic and intellect exceeded that role. Our CFO had retired, and instead of bringing in another person, I worked to mentor Melanie across various roles. She grew to lead as the financial controller responsible for virtually all aspects of our finances. The other, Eric LeBow, was young, energetic and great with people. Our managed-services group was small, but Brett and I saw a chance to expand that business line, and we thought Eric was the right fit for building a team and putting a process in place. Within a few years, he grew managed services to account for almost 50 percent of the company's revenue and went on to become President of Spanlink.

Nurturing talent is given a lot of lip service but is often overlooked in the midst of the day's workload and the rush to get it done. I have learned that spending time identifying people to take on greater roles and responsibilities pays off for everyone involved and, more important, it strengthens the institution.

As well as we were doing during this period, there were, at times, serious challenges.

Relatively early on, our lead banker called up one day and said, "We're going to have to cut your line of credit." The bank, it turned out, was reassessing the risk of all their business customers and, although we were good customers, we did push the envelope when we could to manage cash flow. Our credit line was cut in half—a significant cut for a company that was building such complex systems for its customers. We had to carefully manage the time between when we ordered equipment and the time a customer paid for it.

My immediate reaction was, "You can't do this! We're a good customer, and we have built up a relationship of trust."

After that conversation, the banker gave us back a little more credit, but it wasn't what we needed. What I needed to do was convince the banker to give us more.

In a follow-up discussion, I offered the bank this deal: "We're going to give you the metrics that we're going to deliver against every month, and if we deliver on the metrics, you're going to get our credit back to where it was, and in this time period." The bank agreed, I believe, because I emphasized that "this isn't a transaction—this is a long-term relationship." They'd been working with us for three or four years.

The key aspect, I think, was that I'd said to them, "As I earn back credit, you're going to expand it, and if you don't, I'll leave today." I had given them a choice: Did they want to invest in the relationship or limit the risk of the relationship? We wound up staying with them and they with us. Within six months, we got back to the credit level where we'd been, then saw our line of credit double within a year.

Realizing that our reduced credit limit could have significantly impacted the business—and significantly slowed our growth—we knew we now had to be leaner and even more efficient. Brett and I took the opportunity to reset the tone of the business, creating a sense of urgency that focused everyone on the highly leveraged actions that drove more alignment and synchronicity in the business. We held a team meeting to figure out how the plan I'd suggested was going to be executed and what impact it would have. We said, "This is our strategy, and this is our moment. We can either hide in the corner or we can stand out there and fight." The basic message was that we weren't going to be taken advantage of anymore—not by competitors, customers, suppliers, vendors or even employees. We were a good company that built great products and had a solid culture, and we were going to stand up and fight for what we believed. We needed to preserve what many had created. In retrospect, thanks to the bank's initial action, we ended up being stronger than before.

There was a lot to defend. We had undertaken some of the largest and most innovative rollouts of VoIP systems in the U.S. and abroad and had some of the biggest customers in the world: Maryland Procurement Office (aka NSA), Aetna, Gateway, Travelers Insurance, Wells Fargo, EchoStar, Harley-Davidson, Corporate Express, W.W. Grainger, the State of Minnesota. We installed and maintained the systems to manage all of their contact centers.

The State of Minnesota was an interesting case study, and it was a success story not only for Spanlink but for the state itself.

The state had some 29 or more separate departments all running their own individual systems. The Minnesota state government had been hearing from constituents that the quality of customer care was lacking. Through VoIP technologies, we were asked to find a way to treat those separate departments as one, unified network, saving the state a lot of money and bringing a lot more efficiency to how agencies talked to one another, shared information and enhanced the customer experience. We did that for the Minnesota Department of Revenue, the DMV and all the other state agencies, providing them with a best-in-class system.

In effect, the Minnesota government became its own telephone-service provider, keeping those monies within the state instead of paying an outside provider, like AT&T or Verizon. The state's IT department became the telephone provider, and the disparate offices were able to pay themselves as a result of us creating a revenue opportunity and great cost savings for them. It was incredibly transformative for a government to do this, and Minnesota was one of the first states to do so. It was also an example of Cisco's belief in how digital technologies can create connected governments and connected cities, transforming them—and businesses—in the process. This is just one of many examples through which I learned about how digital strategies can improve the efficiency of state and local governments.

The real eye-opener for me in this phase of my career, however, was that there were vibrant ecosystems outside of Silicon Valley.

Before Suzanne, Kayden and I moved there, I heard people reference Minnesota as a fly-over state. In reality, it's a robust economic environment that has produced great companies for more than a century—companies like General Mills, Land O'Lakes, Target and Federal Express. The nation's first enclosed retail mall, Rosedale Center, was in Minnesota, an innovation that reflected how people wanted to live and shop. Leaders in the state created this Midwest ecosystem around their own culture, values, weather and climate. They had done things well in healthcare and biotech- devices industries, as well as in the food and retail spaces, and so were able to play off the capabilities and competencies that they had acquired.

There are many places that have been able to create ecosystems for businesses. In the case of Minnesota, it did it with a vibrant art and culture scene, good restaurants and diverse populations. Silicon Valley doesn't hold a patent on innovation. Human work ethic, imagination and entrepreneurism are geographically independent. It just takes the right ingredients to allow people to innovate and compete. What's needed in a given region are applied-research universities, people willing to invest capital to grow businesses and a cost of living that can support people of all economic means. You also need an urban environment that allows people to live in density—80 percent of Minnesota's population lives within 80 miles of Minneapolis—so that they interact with other people and exchange ideas. Ecosystems require a vibrant business community of entrepreneurs as well as small, medium and large businesses supported by networks of tradespeople and professionals who keep the engines going.

We're seeing ecosystems of that kind develop today in areas as widespread as Austin, Texas; Haifa, Israel; and Bangalore, India. Around the world, business and government leaders are using a similar formula: They are finding what they're good at and who their people are, and then they're asking, "How do we educate those citizens and get people to invest in them in order to support and grow business?" That's the winning combination—and the future—for any city, state or region.

A lot of what we did with Cisco and Spanlink was showing people what their future could be. We developed executive briefing centers equipped with the latest technology to show how it could change people's worlds. It's one thing for people to read about technology and another for them to actually put their hands on something and understand how it works: "Oh, so *this* is how I can order a pizza through my TV!" We showed them how a customer having a problem with their refrigerator could text the manufacturer and get an instantaneous call back from a call-center agent. The agent, in real time, would be given performance data on the refrigerator from the "smart" system to help diagnose and solve the customer's problem remotely, getting information fed to him by a smart system that knows both the customer and the requested information. As remarkable at the time was that the transcript of the customer-agent interaction would then be sent to a supervisor in order to train the agent and improve the process. This all may sound basic and fundamental now, but, back then, these were all ideas of fiction.

A good example of Spanlink's value added involved W.W. Grainger, the Fortune 500 industrial-supply company founded in Chicago in 1927 that serves as a kind of Costco or Home Depot for tradespeople. The company had 500 locations across 50 states and, just like the state of Minnesota's offices, none of them were communicating with one another. When we heard that, it was like music to our ears because we knew what they needed and how to implement it.

The example we used to show the benefits of our technology was this: Say a Polish-speaking customer living in Boston wanted to talk to someone who also spoke Polish when he called his local Grainger store, however, there was no one in the store who spoke Polish. Well, the caller's question in Polish would be understood by our system and immediately routed to a W.W. Grainger store in Chicago or Texas or another location. All of a sudden, you would have the Polish-speaking customer talking to a Polish-speaking representative who could answer questions.

The solution, it seemed clear to us, was to integrate all 500 of the company's branches into one virtual store. By having not just the right people but the most knowledgeable person available to customers, those retail branches could effectively become call centers and improve the customer experience. In the end, it was about paying attention to the customer—a lesson we had learned early on.

In our first big presentation of the solution to Grainger, with Brett Shockley leading the Spanlink sales team, Grainger's CIO and CTO (Chief Information Officer and Chief Technology Officer, respectively) weren't really getting our concept. And it was critical that they did because, along with Cisco, we were in competition with two other, larger companies for Grainger's business. It was at that point that Brett took over the show and began explaining what we were trying to do. He was masterful at understanding the voice of the customer and, using the customers' own words, articulating what they really needed and getting them to buy. Often a sales team will miss what a customer is saying because the team doesn't realize that the process is less about what it has to sell and more about what the customer wants to buy. Which is why Brett would always say, "You have to keep the voice of the customer." It was similar to Hal Kruth saying, "Keep people at the center in your value proposition."

At any rate, the end result of Brett's performance in that meeting was that Grainger decided to throw this huge project to us rather than to the major competition. They understood that ours was the right solution and, more importantly, that we were the right people to get the job done within the required timeframe. That gave us a big vote of confidence, especially after having our credit cut only a year earlier. In the end, Brett's ability to show the customer we understood their needs, along with our ability to execute on the solution, is what sealed the deal. And it was also because Grainger's CIO and other executives saw that we were aligned as a team in what we were doing, and they trusted that we were the ones to deliver not only the solution but the benefits, too.

After the rigorous evaluation period and "bake-off" between the other vendors, we had won the deal. Now, we had to execute the contract, which was a couple of hundred pages in length, and it was the thickest thing I'd ever seen. I had the privilege of flying out to Grainger's company headquarters in Lake Forest, Illinois. For three weeks straight, I'd arrive there at 8 a.m. and stay until 8 p.m.—12-hour days negotiating with Grainger's procurement person and an outside counsel—then go back to the hotel. John Semion, my CFO, worked with me on every detail of the contract, which was important to Grainger because in digitalizing their phone service through which customers ordered, they were potentially putting their entire business potentially at risk. They wanted to be absolutely sure they had a contract that was going to live up to their expectations.

In effect, it was three weeks of understanding Grainger's needs, assessing the risks, mitigating as much of that risk as we could and ultimately getting to a place where we could sign a contract with Grainger's CEO. In the end, the relationship we created with Grainger helped build a strong foundation that, in turn, led to the successful completion of our project with them. We spent the better part of six months working seven days a week to deliver what Grainger needed. It was very demanding and tested our mettle.

This project was so impactful and well executed that the Grainger CEO described it as the most transformational information-technology project of his tenure. It was also a testament to how a small, innovative company can help transform a much larger customer. We heard that the results of this effort added over $800 million of value to the company. Not bad for the impact of a small company. This was an incredible demonstration of the teamwork and dedication of the engineers and deployment team at Spanlink.

In 2004, our second daughter, Kira, was born. Unlike the complexities of Kayden's birth, Kira came easily and was healthy. I cherished the next two years we spent as a family. We were a small family learning about a new city with time just to be together. Don't get me wrong—balancing two kids three and under was no walk in the park, but Suzanne and I learned a lot about each other in the process. It was a fun time, yet we slowly came to the realization that we wanted a change. We'd been fortunate enough to do some interesting things in our lives that involved new locations—Philadelphia, Boston, San Francisco, Minneapolis—because we'd always been chasing jobs and careers. Now, Suzanne and I started having conversations that involved questions like, "When are we going to take more control so we can set down roots? Where do we want that to be?" As much as we enjoyed our experiences in various cities, our roots were in Connecticut. Both our parents were on the East Coast, and we'd always imagined eventually coming back to the Nutmeg State to raise our family and grow our careers. The public schools had worked for us, and we wanted to be closer to family. We wanted our parents to be involved in our kids' lives. We also missed friends, the culture of Connecticut, the seasons and the people.

Brett and I had many conversations about the needs of the business and opportunities to expand. I realized through our discussions that for us to get to the next level, I had to re-up, as they say in the military, and stay in Minnesota with the company for another five years—that's what the business needs called for—or it was time to go back to Connecticut. Suzanne and I weighed the pros and cons and did a bit of an audit of what we wanted for our family. That's when we made the decision that it was time to come back home.

LESSONS LEARNED

- Business is about people and relationships. These interactions strengthen when people are able to come together and spend time together solving problems.

- Understand and embrace the advances in technology at the risk of getting left behind. We must improve educational outcomes to ensure opportunity for everyone.

- Nurture talent by investing in the people around you to strengthen an organization. None of us is permanent in any role and we have to leave an institution stronger than how we found it.

Chapter 10

COMING BACK HOME TO CONNECTICUT

T hey say timing is everything. Well, coming home to Connecticut when I did does seem to have always been in the cards. Frankly, like rubber bands, many decisions had been pulling me back here all along.

After graduating from the Naval Academy, I could have chosen any one of four nuclear-reactor prototypes in the country for training: South Carolina, where the winters are warmer than in the Northeast; Idaho, where one could ski practically year-round; and upstate New York. But I chose Windsor in northern Connecticut. Later, I moved to Groton for Naval Submarine School. Obviously, marrying Suzanne Tager in Wilton attached another string to home. Actually, we made the move to Connecticut for the family and friends we wanted to be around. It was the place we wanted to raise our family.

So, in July of 2005, I left Spanlink and Minneapolis, we sold our house, I sold my car and we moved in temporarily with Suzanne's parents in Westport, Connecticut. Overnight, three generations were under one roof. As a sailor and submariner, it challenged my sense of organization, but it was good to be back home in Connecticut!

Although my daughters, Kayden and Kira, really don't remember much of that period in their lives, it was a valuable experience for them, and for Suzanne and me. We often talk about that time when all six of us were living together. It serves as a lesson of how family members can and should support each other and the gratitude and thanks we need to give in return.

I got down to work trying to envision my future. Honestly, the easy career decision for me at the time would probably have been to go back to California. Aside from the fact that that's where my brothers and their families were, my Silicon Valley network of engineers, team members and friends was there. Yet Connecticut was where we wanted to be, and it was what we wanted for our kids. We ended up settling in a home down the road from my in-laws. We said, "Whatever comes, this is where we were meant to be, and this is where we're going to make our home."

With the family finally settled, I got on with figuring out my next career step. I started networking in the community with people I had known and making cold calls to job recruiters and local business people. But at that time, in 2005, there were not a lot of technology jobs to be had, or even high-tech companies in New York City, let alone Connecticut. I went to Hartford to meet with various folks in industry and government but just didn't find anything that was right for me. I was met with "That is really cool what you've done, but we don't have a lot of software companies here." I traveled to Boston to meet with companies there and found more opportunities, but I did not want to put myself or my family through a weekly commute again. Besides, the number of opportunities were just so small compared to other regions. Don't get me wrong—there were a few good technology-focused companies around, like Priceline, Kayak and Tangoe, but I just did not find the right thing for me. To this day, I am impressed with how these companies have been able to grow and compete against their better-supported, out-of-state rivals.

When you spend time in Silicon Valley, or even in Minneapolis, you get a sense of the ecosystems that support themselves. The foundation of growth emanates from the applied-research universities and research organizations that create new technologies, and the corporations, small and large, that work together with these organizations to bring new technology to market. This results in the hiring of more employees and the need for supporting industries like investors, lawyers and the like. This growth in jobs must then be matched with an increase in trade workers, retail and transportation to meet the needs of the area. You can literally see the changes brought about by an economy that is driving growth. My perspective was from that of the technology industry, but the results of a successful economy are the same—whether it is in the financial district of New York City or the movie business in Hollywood.

Despite the presence in Connecticut of a few successful tech companies, there weren't enough of them, nor was there support from the state's leaders to encourage innovation and technology across industries. However, as so often happens when you've worked hard and have created good working relationships with others, conversations lead to opportunities—especially when an ecosystem and exciting opportunities are lacking at home.

So, not long after moving back to Connecticut, I got a call one day from Norman Winarsky, who had taken over for Hal Kruth as head of ventures and licensing at SRI International. I had worked closely with Norman on both Discern and Spanlink. Norman himself is an accomplished engineer and researcher who worked for years at the famous Sarnoff Corporation in Princeton. He is actually one of the few people I know who has solved Maxwell's equations, which describe how electric charges and currents work together. Many of us engineering students try, but few succeed. While at Sarnoff, he and Curt Carlson, CEO of SRI, were instrumental in creating the high-definition TV standard which we all use today.

Norman had been working on the next inventions to commercialize from SRI and reached out to me. After talking with Curt, he said to me, "Steve, we have some technologies we're assessing and would love to have you come back and be a venture advisor—and maybe you'll even head up one of them as a CEO for us again."

This meant, of course, that I'd have to go back to California during the week. It was something I didn't want to do, but the chance of working again with the world-class researchers and developers at SRI was hard to resist. Sadly, this is what was missing in Connecticut—not the companies or workforce, but the mentality and drive to build a vibrant ecosystem that would, in turn, create a high-tech corridor to rival Massachusetts and any other state. The fact of the matter is that Connecticut has smart, ambitious people. It has great institutions of higher education, an abundance of resources, solid infrastructure and enviable transportation close to arguably the center of the world when it comes to industry, finance and intellectual and creative capital. Yet the leadership in Hartford was listless, and not only unable or unwilling to pull these assets together but seemingly doing their best to push them away!

In spite of my reservations, I began flying out to Menlo Park, California, every other week and, between trips, working from home. On my first visit back, I saw Curt Carlson in the hallway. Curt, who is something like 6'3", came right toward me and gave me a big handshake. He adjusted his glasses back to the bridge of his nose—they famously drift down to the tip from time to time—and declared, "So, you are back to build a billion-dollar company with us!" Norman and I got to work looking at various technologies and market-mapping them. I was able to walk the labs again and sit down with engineers and scientists. Two of my favorites were in the Artificial Intelligence Lab: Doug Appelt, whose wife administered the website addresses in the early days of the Internet, and Mabry Tyson, who was a prodigious software researcher on many important projects for SRI. Both were top-notch researchers that were instrumental in developing the core technology that Discern was all about. I talked to them and others about what they were working on and the state of readiness for the commercial market. After I had a good understanding of our capability, I reached out to people in various companies and industries to seek more information on their challenges and problems.

The goal was to match problems with solutions. Some of the things we looked at were big ideas like a search engine that we called "Grok" that indexed every video in the world—remember, this was 2005 and YouTube was created in February of that year—to something as simple as aligning the text of a book or song to an audio file. Companies like Amazon and Google were interested in this capability. Say someone was reading their book before bed and went to sleep. Then, when that person got into the car to go to work, he or she could pick up with the audio book in the same place. Think of it as bookmarking an audio file. Let's just say neither idea went further for several reasons as we went through the innovation process.

One of the three or four ideas and opportunities we had in the works at the time was something called Siri. To remind you, I had looked at it back in 2000 before Discern was started, but the concept was just premature at that time. Both Discern and SRI were technologies developed out of the Artificial Intelligence Lab at SRI International. Between 2000 and 2005, the U.S. DARPA had been focusing on a big problem that required AI expertise: it wanted soldiers of the future, who would be in the field with their hands on their weapons and triggers, to be able to use their voices to call up and say, "Pull up a map of Anbar Province," or, "Call the commander of Squadron 3." It called this project CALO, or "Cognitive Assistant that Learns and Organizes," from the Latin *calonis*, which translates to "soldier's servant." DARPA created the program to study the problem and solutions, and SRI was the project manager of the program, pulling together over 300 people across 25 universities and research organizations. Beyond SRI, the other teams were from Stanford University, Yale University, Carnegie Mellon University, the University of Rochester, MIT, the University of Massachusetts at Amherst, and the University of Southern California, among others. Did you realize that Yale had a hand in what turned into Siri? This was a big, bold initiative and a success for the U.S. military, but it also transformed the world in general with many innovative new products we all now use every day.

Key to this effort was the ability to allow people to use their voice, by means of an object-oriented programming language, to interface with many different databases easily and receive answers to their questions. Originally, the program was called OAA, or Open Agent Architecture. This effort was led by a researcher and engineer named Adam Cheyer, who had been working on OAA for ten-plus years. Adam is technically talented and has great vision for the future. He showed me a really compelling demonstration of a groundbreaking program that he had developed. He had taken OAA, a bunch of "software agents" that interact with different databases—say, information for restaurants, movies, etc.—and then built a speech-interface on the front to access the data. I walked into his office and he showed me all of this using a Compaq IPAQ, one of the first pocket PCs of its time and originally released in 2000. Using the system, Adam could either type in or speak a question—for example, "What Italian restaurants have a table available for four people at 7 p.m. in Palo Alto?"—and it would go to a server, then deliver an answer. Initially, the system was called "Hal" as a reference to Arthur Clarke's Space Odyssey Series and the fictional talking computer Hal 9000, and the name evolved to "Siri" in reference to the Norse meaning "beautiful woman who leads you to victory."

The team at SRI International said to me, "There's a sizeable market out there, Steve, and a real need for this product. The future of computing will require that people can access all this expanding information easily with their voice. We need you to find that market." Over the course of the next year, I went around to perhaps 75 of the top technology and telecom companies in the world, and the door slammed closed every time. "Why do we need this?," they all asked. *Boom!* This was at the time when Google was really getting traction, and I said, "But you'll be able to compete against Google with this!" And their response was, "Nah. We don't need that feature. Speech recognition doesn't work anyway." (Many of these companies, it's interesting to note, are shadows of themselves today.) As a team, we worked our butts off on this. As Adam Cheyer has noted, "In those early days, the Siri team worked long and hard to validate our vision and dial in our market value proposition. As a founding member of Siri, Steve was key in translating our unique capability into a commercial offering that we could take to market." But those early days were frustrating, for sure. There was so much potential for Siri but, like many cutting-edge ideas, the conditions for success often take time to catch up with the product. Siri was no exception.

This was now 2006. Apple's iPhone didn't launch until the following year. As I said before, in many ways life is about timing. Sometimes you have to be patient and wait for shifts in markets and technology before an innovative new product or service takes hold. Or as my friend, Manish Sabharwal from Wharton, always reminds me, "You can't force a plant from a seed." You do have to work hard and challenge the reality of markets, time and technology, but sometimes Mother Nature has her own timeline. That was my lesson from DIVA and Discern. We all knew that miniaturization of technology was accelerating and that smartphones were coming—first the PalmPilot, then the Trio—which were successes in their own right. Siri at that point had some limitations. The devices weren't powerful enough, for one thing, but once we had a reliable smartphone or device, things would be different. The phones would be better and much quicker. I knew this, and so did the team at Siri. Again, it would just take time for the tech industry at large to catch up with us.

Meanwhile, no one was breaking down our door to buy Siri back then. It was clear from Curt Carlson and Norm Winarsky that for Siri to be a success, or simply for us to carry on, it was time to spin off the program and create a separate company from SRI International. This is what Adam Cheyer had wanted all along. The next question for me came from Norman: "So, Steve," he said, "when are you moving back to California so we can get started?"

It had been a conversation between Norman and me for a while: When would I move out to Menlo Park? With the investment and decisions that we were going to be making, I knew what the job required in terms of focus, attention and time to be successful. From my viewpoint living in Connecticut, I also knew it was going to be a five- to six-year commitment to have a shot at making any company, let alone one like Siri, successful. In my experience, I have found that there are no enduring overnight success stories in business. Building companies and creating real jobs takes time and a whole lot of hard work. As a result, it is my opinion that going into any new job or company takes a mental commitment of at least five to ten years.

Suzanne and I had several long conversations in which we weighed the pros and cons of staying in Connecticut versus moving back to California. We had a feeling that a move out West would probably keep us there for good, and we didn't like that feeling. Still, I knew that Siri was a great technology and product. I was proud of how SRI as a company kept investing in the future and how the Artificial Intelligence Center—led in this case by Adam Cheyer's vision and tireless efforts— had crafted a great team. From a career perspective, my decision should have been simple: We were working on some of the coolest, leading-edge technology that would eventually change how people communicate. This type of work has been a big focus of my technology career. The trends pointed to smart phones that would become pervasive. A final key piece was machine-learning techniques that started to be applied to speech-recognition systems, which would make these systems work for consumers. The potential was incredible.

So, it was an especially hard decision from the heart, given that two of my brothers, Paul and Jim, along with their families, were out West.

The closeness in age of all of our kids had some allure as well—having cousins being able to grow up together in the same area. And yet, there was that old gravitational pull Suzanne and I felt to be here. After weighing everything, we knew we wanted to stay in Connecticut. This was home. This is where we wanted to be.

I went to Norman Winarsky and Curt Carlson, explaining my decision. That was not a fun conversation, realizing that my time working with SRI might be over. I believe strongly that even in this current trend toward remote workers, people need to be in the same room solving problems, especially in an early-stage company. The right thing for the business was to bring leadership to Siri and the other ventures SRI was working on in Menlo Park. SRI went on to hire a great first-time CEO, Dag Kittlaus, from Motorola. He and Tom Gruber rounded out the founding team, and they later added key engineering talent including SRI alumni such as Chris Brigham, Didier Guzzoni, and Rich Giuli. Siri executed very well on its initial product and caught the eye of Apple—as I had guessed, it took several years for Apple to see the value of Siri before buying it in 2010. Adam, Dag and Chris eventually left Apple and started Viv, which focused on the original vision of SRI. That product is now Samsung's response to Siri. Even Apple did not fully execute Adam's full vision of what he wanted to accomplish back in 2005.

Helen Mirren, the actress, once said, "You write your life story by the choices you make." She's right. There were times back then when I wished I could have continued with SRI. The work there captured so much of my mind and interests, but my heart was here. Although it was a hard realization that it was time to move on from SRI, something in my gut told me this was where we were supposed to be, and I was committed to finding a way to make the kind of opportunities SRI presented possible in our area. Little did I know that my friend, Michael Summers, would call about a cool technology he came across that was used for submarines, one that he wanted to use for mobile networks to make cellphones work more reliably.

Closing doors is hard, but it allows for others to open down the road. And they were about to open right here in Connecticut for me.

LESSONS LEARNED

- Home should not just be where our families are but where we find the opportunities to pursue our passions and careers while positively impacting our communities.

- To make a state or region viable to attract people today requires applied-research universities that create new ideas and solutions working in concert with businesses, small and large, to get new ideas to market to change people's lives.

- There are no enduring overnight-success stories in business. Building companies and creating real jobs take time and a whole lot of hard work.

Chapter 11

CREATING JOBS FOR THE FUTURE

Ernest Hemingway once said, "The best way to find out if you can trust somebody is to trust them," and I agree. Trust is the foundation of any successful relationship, be it between two people, a team of people or a community of people. Creating and fostering an environment where trust can flourish is something I have focused on more and more the older I have gotten. I have learned that trust is one of those intangible forces, like compounded interest, that prevents problems and allows people to reach a level of achievement beyond what they believe possible. To me, there are three key ingredients that have to be in place to grow trust:

Fairness: If people are treated fairly, they feel that they can commit to and help improve that relationship with an individual or as part of a broader community.

Openness: Fairness allows people to be open to sharing their ideas and providing and accepting feedback to help strengthen the overall group.

Truth: Only when people feel they are well treated and can share openly does a consensus of truth arise that aligns a team, business or community to achieve great things.

I often have put these principles, along with values and a vision for an organization, on a small, pocket-sized card for each person in my businesses to keep handy. Creating, establishing and growing trust is an ongoing, dynamic process. Once this process goes into motion, it creates a flywheel that provides greater stability and power to address obstacles and overcome challenges. In my opinion, great teams that achieve success build trust not only between themselves but with their customers and other stakeholders. When done right, the process creates "perpetual energy": as a team keeps delivering benefits for its customers, people trust one another more, which keeps them together longer and motivates them to accomplish more things together. Early in my career, I learned a lot about building and managing teams both large and small. I often tried in those early days to do too much myself. But I grew to realize that learning to build teams and rely on other people makes companies stronger. I believe we have to learn to complement our blind spots by valuing what others bring to the table in order to be successful as leaders and as organizations.

Little did I know that these overlapping concepts of trust as perpetual energy and valuing and relying on others were to prove to be so important to my next business!

In June of 2006, I got a call from Michael Summers, my old friend and colleague from SRI. "I'm here in England working with Hal Kruth, who's now chief operating officer of Qinetiq," Michael said. (Qinetiq, a play on the word "kinetic," as in energy, is a very similar company in mission to SRI, but based in the United Kingdom. Today, Qinetiq is a multinational research and development organization.) "Hal has a small division with great potential," Michael went on, "and we want to launch it as a standalone company. Given our previous work together, we thought that you would be a good fit to head it. Are you up for another adventure?"

Intrigued, as an entrepreneur with an engineering mindset would be, I flew to London the following week to meet with Michael and Hal. I was briefed on the nascent division, called Quintel Technologies, including the challenges and opportunities ahead, and the following day I drove west of London down the M3 motorway to Farnborough, where Quintel was then located.

The Quintel team had come up with several unique applications to dramatically increase the efficiency of cellular networks that power mobile phones. At the core of their large set of patents was a key one that was actually based on a sonar technique for submarines. Quintel's key technologist, Dave Barker, had adapted it to improve cellular networks since sound signals in water and air exhibit many of the same attributes. From Manchester, England, Dave looked like Paul McCartney of the Beatles with his cropped dark hair and ever-present, knee-length black jacket with the collar turned up, and he is one of the most intelligent people I have ever worked with. Dave has a way of seeing things in four dimensions and making connections across disciplines that I have difficulty envisioning sometimes. There were many conversations I would have with Dave where he would literally stretch and expand my mind, to such a degree, I'd end up with a massive headache!

What I found when I got to Farnborough was a product that had two main parts. There was a huge gray box that sat on the ground that was five feet high and three feet wide, filled with expensive filters and electronics, along with three eight-foot-tall antennas that get mounted on top of a cell tower. When I asked the cost to build the product, the answer was almost $30,000 per location. And that was the cost, not the price! But at the time, it offered the best solution by far than any other. I was rapidly tossing questions at the team and challenging their thinking. In that initial meeting, the Quintel team looked at me in an unsure manner, not entirely trusting me at first. Here I am with a Silicon Valley mindset coming in to assess a British team. It was something I knew I had to work on as we moved forward.

I went back to London and gave Michael and Hal my observations: "The core team is solid," I told them, "and the technology is interesting. But they haven't found the right market need, and it's way too expensive. It has to be repackaged, miniaturized and made affordable." I also knew that in doing my due diligence for Quintel, cellular companies like Verizon and Sprint spend $150 billion a year on mobile infrastructure to power their networks. I thought, 'If we can carve out a small portion of $150 billion, we will be successful.' No small task but the size of the opportunity seemed too great to pass up. I remembered a quote from Jeff Hawkins, creator of Palm Pilot: "One of the keys to entrepreneurial success is that you must jump headfirst into a new field before it is 100 percent clear you can be successful." I agreed to take on the jobs of chairman and chief executive officer of Quintel with one condition— that my trusted friend and chief financial officer, John Semion, could join me. I knew I needed John on this journey; the trust we had built working on Discern and Spanlink would be needed to navigate not only the Quintel team but working with Qinetiq. As mentioned in the context of Discern, John has the presence of Gandalf from J.R.R. Tolkien's *Lord of the Rings*, and his calm sensibilities. Having worked with John for now 17 years, I find we partner well on starting, growing and turning around businesses. I am not sure there is anyone, other than Suzanne, who has seen me through as many highs and lows of my career.

Discern had taught me how to identify technologies that address real needs, and Spanlink had given me the chance to grow teams and deliver large-scale solutions to demanding customers. Quintel was an opportunity to do both of these in one company.

For me, there was another exciting part of the opportunity. I had a good handle on software and concepts like agile development techniques. Quintel provided a chance for me to learn how to manufacture hardware products in large volume by applying things like lean manufacturing and Six Sigma techniques or process improvement. It was a good thing I had Lindsay Ager, Quintel's COO, who was accomplished in these areas, because I had a lot to learn. Early on, Lindsay highlighted what I believe is potentially the biggest myth of manufacturing—that jobs are lost to overseas because of labor costs. This is undoubtedly the case for some industries, but for us, only eight percent of our costs were for labor, which is a very small percentage in electronics. Lindsay ingrained into my thinking that "materials drive cost." Beyond the cost of labor, manufacturers need to have localized supply chains for materials, cost-effective energy costs and transportation networks to get raw materials in and finished products out to customers.

There was one other very valuable lesson Lindsay helped me realize: states and nations can play an active role in helping to foster a productive environment for manufacturers. The truth of this would become all too apparent, and very soon.

Likewise, states and nations that focus on supply chains for material, transportation, energy and workforce talent can reinvent manufacturing in the 21st century.

So here I was again, on American Airlines every week, making the seven-hour-five-minute flight back and forth between Connecticut and London. And once again, Suzanne and I were juggling raising our daughters, who were three and five years old at the time, managing our own careers and sharing household responsibilities.

In England, it soon became apparent that while the talent and energy were there, the culture was different enough from Silicon Valley—buttoned-up and staid compared to dynamic and free flowing—that it would keep Quintel from achieving its full potential. Also missing was a clear understanding of Quintel's "golden nugget"—the key aspect of a product that induces a customer to buy it.

Here I went back to the NABC value proposition framework I had learned at SRI from Curt Carlson and Hal Kruth. This is what we found:

Need: Mobile-phone companies had to add more and more antennas on tens of thousands of towers and change them out every seven to ten years. That took a lot of coordination, labor and time.

Approach: Quintel had a unique, patented ability to effectively get the output of ten antennas out of one antenna, with the additional ability to control each signal independently.

Benefit: Mobile operators could deploy fewer antennas to get the same coverage and capacity for their networks. And they could get more capacity in constrained, high-value areas like New York City and San Francisco.

Competition: Our only competition forced customers to hang more antennas, which would lead to more rental costs and more antennas to buy. In many places, like urban areas, this was not practical.

In summary, Quintel's "golden nugget" was its ability to get ten times the capacity out of traditional cellular antennae. Quintel had previously launched a product using this capability so that several cellular companies could share one antenna. Vodafone, Orange and a few other U.K. companies were actually sharing that huge, expensive product but adoption was slow. I just didn't have a good feeling about using the current product going forward. To validate the real market need, I was able to recruit Joe Veni, a hard-nosed telecom sales executive and Brooklyn native who had long since moved to California. Joe knew how to sell to cellular companies, and I learned a lot from him. His first step was ensuring that his customers trusted him. Trust is a necessary ingredient to speed up the sales cycle. I remember that he and I had an early meeting with AT&T and asked them about their need for a specific "sharing product" that Vodafone and others were using. They were pretty clear in their response: "We don't share with other operators." At first, we were deflated, but they then said, "However, similar to sharing we have 2G, 3G and upcoming 4G networks that could all go on one antenna. Can you do that?" Joe and I looked at each other and then almost in harmony turned to them and said, "Of course, we can do that." That meeting was a turning point and defined how we could apply our golden nugget to the U.S. wireless market.

We went back to the drawing board and got to work designing smaller, more powerful and less expensive antennas. This gave cellular operators like Verizon and AT&T more capacity and flexibility, which meant they had to buy fewer antennas and rent less cell-tower space. Now, all we had to do was manufacture our products and make them a reality.

When we launched, Quintel was challenged by many in the

industry who thought our concept was nothing more than a crazy idea. No one had innovated cellular antennae in 20 years. What made us unique is that we were fairly certain we could pull it off! I tried to create in our team a sense of purpose and of destiny—that we could build a strong institution and that success was on our side. We could change the landscape of mobile networks. It would take strong leadership, a unifying vision, a focus on shared result and the ability to stretch a buck along the way. There were headwinds, for sure, but I have found that all successful ideas go through three phases of commercial challenge before adoption: ridicule, opposition, self-evidence. We had met the first, with people saying, "You're crazy even to try this." The second phase comes when you produce an actual product or service, but people think of reasons why they shouldn't use it. And the third is when you're successful; that's when the critics acknowledge that this is the way it was supposed to be!

In the early days, Quintel was doing some key manufacturing on the eastern shore of Maryland, of all places. It turns out there's a good density of cellular-equipment manufacturers there, but Quintel was too far away to work tightly with our suppliers and contract manufacturers. Ultimately, we came to the decision that the business wasn't going to grow as long as it was in England, and that design and manufacturing had to be close to the company.

Meanwhile, as word spread about Quintel, non-government organizations and government entities alike began to reach out to us. It was obvious they wanted to attract high-tech companies that could support high-wage workers. Officials from the Chinese government called and said, "Move your business to China. We'll give you manufacturing space in the Guangdong Province and free electricity!" The Infocomm Development Authority (IDA) of Singapore, one of the country's economic planning agencies, wanted us to move there, and the European Bank of Reconstruction and Development wanted us to set up manufacturing in Hungary!

What I took away from this proactive outreach was the length to which countries went in order to attract innovative companies. They would make extensive pitches for their location, talented work force and commitment to innovation. If countries were aggressively recruiting us, I reasoned, why not see if Connecticut was a good place for us? After all, aside from being close to home for me, at one time, Connecticut enjoyed an extraordinary manufacturing capability. Around World War II, 80 percent of our state's economy had been driven by defense spending. In fact, we still have superior submarine and helicopter manufacturers, along with the machine shops and financial services to support them, and, until recently, we had been a leading manufacturer of many durable products. We had always been an entrepreneurial state. Why couldn't we become a leader in cellular products? Why couldn't we help build a whole new ecosystem around the software and hardware of the future?

I soon found out why.

The discussions we had with people in Connecticut that year were frustrating. There wasn't a sense of what was going on outside of the state or a sense of urgency to understand our needs and match them with resources in Connecticut. People in other countries—in China and Singapore and Hungary—had understood, but the people at home just didn't get it.

Besides a lack of understanding when it came to Quintel's needs and what we wanted to do, there was a noticeable lack of energy and desire here to recreate the kinds of ecosystems, infrastructure and partnerships among the key components in the state: government, universities, business and technology. And ecosystems, I learned from my time in Silicon Valley, are critically important.

The more complex the world gets, and the more complex products get, the more businesses need teams of people who are expert in different areas to work together. For most companies, it is not possible or affordable to hire all that expertise. Why is Hollywood the center of the movie industry? Why does Silicon Valley focus on technology? Why is New York City the hub of financial services, and why did Hartford attract insurance? It's because geographical areas gain benefits when firms and people locate near each other. In order to create new ideas, people with similar focus and expertise come together, which attracts other people who want to work with them. Then, investors are needed to fund these efforts, accountants are needed to monitor the finances and lawyers are key to negotiating contracts. Next, it takes academic institutions to educate young people who will need jobs after graduation and want to go work in these companies, and finally it takes a government that wants to keep these new hires in the state because they pay taxes, plant roots, start families and contribute to the health and well-being of the economy and culture and quality of life.

What my teammates and I at Quintel discovered our company needed, and what we'd found lacking in Connecticut, turned out—of all places—to be across the border in New York State. We were introduced to government officials in Albany. They were aggressively looking to attract technology and manufacturing businesses to the state. We told them what we needed: access to applied-research universities, a talented workforce, good cost of living and a welcoming manufacturing environment. Through them, we were directed upstate to Rochester, which had a recovering ecosystem to replace the one from the former heyday of Kodak and Xerox and many of the elements needed to nurture new ideas and young companies. It wasn't perfect, but we saw potential and a place that welcomed us.

The Rochester Institute of Technology and the University of Rochester were two applied-research universities that had readily available professors and students with whom we could partner in order to improve our technology. They were excited to engage with Quintel. There was also a sizeable workforce of talented and highly educated people—men and women with master's degrees and PhDs—who were available due to the downsizing at Xerox and Kodak and a number of contract manufacturers experienced in designing and producing prototypes.

For us at Quintel, dealing with New York was a far better experience than the one we had in Connecticut. In general, states are better served in the long run by investing resources that keep the cost of living competitive and investing in infrastructure that attracts job creators. This should be done through bringing together and highlighting the state's or region's strengths and comparative advantages. And these qualities should be matched to the clusters of companies that currently exist or that are trying to be recruited instead of the kind of glitzy marketing ideas used recently that spend millions on TV ads but do little to attract businesses to a particular area.

The sad realization is that many of the fundamentals to make Connecticut business-friendly to small and large companies already exist in Connecticut. I recently met a residential builder who put it this way: "Connecticut has the right bones in the house, but no one is going to buy it unless it's remodeled and updated."

After a long internal assessment, the Quintel stakeholders decided that Rochester was the right move for the company. The decision created a lot of anxiety for employees for obvious reasons. However, I knew I had gained the employees' trust when, in a critical meeting, I asked who would come with us to Rochester to grow the company, and all of the key people raised their hands! Lindsay Ager, a "royalist" in every good sense of the word, had come to talk to me before the meeting. I thought he was going to be a roadblock to the move—he had a wife and two small children at the time—and I really needed him on the team. He said, "I see greater opportunities for my kids to be educated in the U.S. and better career options for them and me. Let's move to America!" I am fairly certain that if we had not moved Quintel, we would not have been successful. So, our success, in large part, was due to Lindsay's courageous decision for himself and his family. We moved a few core people from England to New York and complemented them with local workers in the Rochester area.

Our move allowed us to build a world-class facility, including a highly specialized anechoic chamber—a room designed to absorb reflections from sound or electromagnetic waves. This was important because you could wait weeks to get into facilities like it—and at great expense—then have to send a team of people there simply to test products. Our test facility was one of only a few in the Northeast. Universities and other companies were interested in using our unique facility, which would only strengthen our relationships further. We also benefited from the local design and manufacturing community, which reduced our lead time to prototype products and shift to volume manufacturing.

Meanwhile, one of the challenges for Quintel was to make certain that our antennas would not only work technically but in harsh environments—temperature extremes, hurricanes, earthquakes—and also over a life expectancy of eight to ten years. Once installed on towers, our antennae would have to stay in place and perform for the entirety of their lifespan. If we placed these antennas across Verizon or AT&T's 60,000 towers and they had to come down for repair or replacement, we'd be out of business. My CFO, John Semion, wouldn't allow us to take that risk. Designing the antenna to required specifications took longer than we expected. Slowly but surely, we reached the standards set by the major cellular operators. I remember a meeting with AT&T when its head of procurement said, "We already have three antenna providers and they are large public or private companies. We don't need a fourth." We had entered the second phase of commercial adoption: opposition. The "FUD Factor" came out in force from competitors as well as from large companies we were trying to sell to (FUD is slang for fear, uncertainty and doubt created by others to put a competitor at a disadvantage). They would give us all the reasons why they shouldn't work with another vendor like us. Thanks largely to Joe Veni, we overcame these objections and focused on the value we brought compared to the vendors already in place.

The initial deployments in Rockford, Illinois, and Tempe, Arizona had their challenges. The drive tests could have shown problems or that signal strength needed to be optimized. These are incredibly complex systems that require a product to work in symphony with other technologies. Whenever we had a problem in the field, I would invoke my friend,

Matt Rochlin, who is fond of saying, "If you don't learn anything from a bad time, it's just a bad time." (My children hear that from me often when they are hitting rough spots.) As we wrestled with design challenges and slipped schedules due to the complexity of our product, we needed one more person to complement the team. We found that person in Dave Piazza, who came in as our head of engineering. Quick-witted and a great engineering leader, Dave focused the product-development resources to put out a high-performing, well-tested set of products. There are a few hires in my life that really made me sleep better at night, and Dave was one of mine. I knew he had exponential potential beyond his role. I do take a large responsibility in helping others to reach their potential, just as Paul Cook and Curt Carlson have done for me. Several years after I left Quintel, Dave eventually filled my role as CEO, and he led it through its successful acquisition by Cirtek. Rightfully, Dave has gone on to lead the combined Quintel-Cirtek team.

The company learned from these challenges, and timing finally became our friend. We learned the importance of three critical aspects of running the business:

- Clear vision of the market's need and our ability to address it;
- Attention to detail in building great products that address the customers' needs and are valued by them; and,
- Working well together as a team that is aligned in purpose and mission, creates a sense of inevitability and fosters team persistence to persevere under all conditions.

Cellular operators had started their migration from 3G to 4G, which requires a refresh of antennas in thousands of locations. The company was ready for the buying wave—we had the right product and the right value proposition that was different from our competition. It had taken time, but as Quintel entered the third and final phase of commercial adoption, and after we started shipping hundreds and thousands of products, our product and concept had become self-evident to our customers. We now hear from them, "We could not do this without Quintel!"

Quintel taught me a lot about growing a global company (one that has now deployed products to over five continents) while helping to power the mobile phones we use every day which have become as valuable as air and water. The foundation of trust we had built around a team that complemented each other was critical to our navigation of these challenging waters. The trust we developed as a team and the customers' satisfaction with our product far exceeded my expectations. I guess it was destiny.

LESSONS LEARNED

- Trust is the intangible force that increases the speed of forming relationships and results.

- Complement your blind spots: Truly value the different skills and DNA of others.

- Be ready to confront and overcome the three phases of commercial acceptance: ridicule, opposition and self-evidence.

- Create a sense of destination and destiny in your team.

Chapter 12

CALL TO SERVE AGAIN

D uring my time with Quintel, a twenty-four-hour trip to India would change my perspective and, in hindsight, my career forever.

In January of 2011, I boarded a plane from Asia to the U.S. and packed myself in the middle row of economy with two people to my left and right for the 16-hour flight home. As we took off, I started to feel what I thought was bronchitis but with an extra tightness in my chest and some general fatigue. I called over a flight attendant to where I was sitting, and did something I had never done in all my years of traveling.

"I've never had to ask this; can you keep an eye on me?" I asked. "I feel like I may be coming down with bronchitis or something."

"Don't worry," she said. "We have a defibrillator and oxygen on board, and there is a doctor a few rows up as well. You'll be okay."

But I wasn't okay. The pain in my chest increased over the next three hours, then it leveled off for the rest of the flight. This plane was en route to Chicago's O'Hare Airport, where I would catch a connecting flight to LaGuardia in New York City. After the plane finally landed in Chicago and as I was disembarking, the same flight attendant came up to me and said, "They have a medical clinic in O'Hare. Do you want to see a medic or a doctor?"

"No, thanks," I said. "I'm going to get home."

Catching an earlier flight than planned, I was picked up at LaGuardia in New York by Frank Ward, who usually took me back and forth to the airport. From the car, I called my doctor, who told me to come in later that day.

"I think I really should be seen," I insisted.

"Well, if you think it's that important, then go to the hospital."

That's when Frank intervened. "Is there a walk-in clinic you can go to?," he asked me, but, when I tried them and the phone line was busy, he took matters into his own hands.

"Forget this!," he said. "I'm taking you to *my* doctor." Twenty minutes later, he had me at his walk-in clinic, grabbed a doctor he knew and said, "You've gotta see this guy right now."

Within 30 seconds of running an EKG, an electrocardiogram, on me to check my heart, the doctor announced, "You have a pulmonary embolism. You have to go to the hospital immediately."

"Okay. Frank can drive me to the hospital," I told her.

"Sure," she responded— "if you want your heart to explode!"

Even Frank, a really good driver, was concerned for my life at this point. *"I'm* not taking you," he said. I had no idea of the severity of the situation. The nurse called 911, and minutes later I was in an ambulance and on my way to Norwalk Hospital.

I spent the next six days in the hospital as a great team of professionals took care of the embolism. It turned out that a few days before my trip to Asia, I had a pretty severe cramp in my right calf muscle, which caused a blood clot. The 16-hour flight to India, plus only being on the ground for a day before heading back home, caused the clot to break free and travel into my lungs. The pain I thought was bronchitis was actually the blood clot in my lungs.

Interestingly enough, this happened around the same time that Serena Williams was stricken with a pulmonary embolism—a sudden blockage of an artery in the lungs caused by blood clots which, if large enough, can be fatal. That a world-class, high-performance athlete like her had been dealt the same health blow but was able to come back from it made me feel a bit better about my prognosis.

For the next several months, I was grounded from flying after doctors advised against it. I did a lot of soul-searching about what I was working on and what was important to me. At that point, I was traveling some three-plus weeks a month with Quintel for our operations in the U.S., Europe and India. We all know that kids are resilient, and my daughters, then nine and seven, had gotten used to my travel schedule. I could tell, though, that my absence had taken a toll on all of us. Suzanne was balancing her career and raising the kids, which put a lot on her shoulders. This episode gave us a chance to think more about what we wanted for our family.

Gradually, the answer became clear. A friend and mentor, Malcolm Pray, once told me, "There are three kinds of people: People who make things happen; people who watch things happen; and people who say what happened." In my opinion, you never want to be caught in that last bucket. My contributions beyond military service and business started to come to the forefront of my mind, and Malcolm's words became almost haunting. With this new perspective, I felt an old familiar urge to figure out how I could serve again.

Suzanne and I both grew up in Connecticut. We were both educated here, and I served in the Navy in Windsor and in Groton. More importantly, I knew what Connecticut was like when I was a kid, I knew what was like now, and I had a good idea of what the state could be in the future.

Meanwhile, serious problems in government and the economy also occurred that year. In the wake of the financial crisis of 2008, and for the first time in history, Standard & Poor's downgraded its outlook on the U.S.'s long-term sovereign debt from stable to negative. Federal Reserve Chairman Ben Bernanke, in an unprecedented meeting with reporters, predicted less economic growth than expected for the year. On August 4, 2011, the Dow plunged 512 points and four days later, another 635 points. To top things off, Connecticut Governor Dannel Malloy, facing a $3.2 billion deficit, went back on one of his campaign promises and raised taxes for every resident in the state, regardless of income.

Aside from family considerations, I began to wonder how I, as an individual, could add value to Connecticut and improve the state for everyone. I talked with Suzanne, my parents, my in-laws and my brothers. My interests and skill sets focused me on the challenges facing Connecticut and our country. One day while I was having lunch with a friend, we spoke about the problems in our state. I got straight to the point and said, "You know, I'm thinking about running for office." He said, "You should. You're what we need, and you should run for Congress." I wasn't sure the U.S. Congress was the logical step. I was honest and said, "I have no idea how to do that." He responded, "I am going to give you a list of 70 people to call. After you've done your homework, you will know if this is something you think you can do and how to approach it."

The idea was to gain a 360-degree view of everything I was going to have to go through as a candidate for Congress. For the next month,

I met with all 70 of the men and women on the list. What I took away from the experience was this: all of the principles I had learned in the Navy and in business could be applied to running a campaign, along with the same degree of discipline that's needed to managing teams and communicating a vision and ideas. Speaking to those folks was the best advice I got. After those 70 conversations, I had figured out what it would take to embark on such a journey.

The most important thing lacking in politics, I learned from them, is leadership. I'm a problem-solver and an engineer at heart. In the Navy and in business, I built, managed and led teams that devised strategies and came up with solutions. I also know what it means to put your own self-interests aside to focus on a common goal.

But first, I had to talk to my old friend Michael Summers from SRI, who was involved with Quintel and sat on the company's board. We came up with a transition plan for me since I was still Quintel's CEO.

I stayed engaged until we found a new CEO who would ensure that our progress would continue in the right direction. After six months, we found a good fit to ensure the successful future of the business. His name was Alastair Westgarth, and he ran Quintel as President and CEO. Alastair did a great job preserving the culture of the organization while taking the business to new levels of success. He later left Quintel in 2016 to head up Google's Project Loon, a network of balloons at the edge of space designed to connect people in rural and remote areas around the world to the Internet. This gave Dave Piazza, the engineering leader, the opportunity to step in as CEO, and he continues in that role today. Amazingly, the management team of Quintel, beyond me and Alastair, has stayed intact over the last decade. This is a testament to our common vision, team cohesion and market success.

Most importantly, hiring Alastair allowed me to focus on my campaign for congress. I created what we called "The Sandwich Tour." I love deli sandwiches, and, as often as my stomach would allow, we would head out to a different deli where I would sit down and just talk to whomever I met. I got in front of a lot of people and heard their challenges and ideas, and I worked to understand their feelings and frustrations. Their frustration with Hartford, in particular, was clear. What I learned was that many of them believed that the career politicians—the ones making policies that affected them, the constituents—lacked real-world experience and a true desire to help average Connecticut residents who, almost to a person, were hard-working men and women. I saw in their eyes and heard in their voices the frustrations they were dealing with each and every day.

Unfortunately, I came up on the short end of that election. But it was a good learning experience and solidified in me the call to serve again in some capacity. I wanted to find a way to work with people in my home state, identify real solutions and figure how to execute them. The process gave me the opportunity to learn a lot and get my ideas in front of a number of people. It also taught me these valuable lessons:

Aim to serve, not just succeed: From a young age, my parents taught me to find ways to serve others with my talents and experiences. Our democratic system survives and thrives on outsiders adding their voices to our civic leadership.

For anything worthwhile, take risks of all kinds: We can't change anything, especially the status quo in government, without taking risks. This requires taking big risks, like organizing a community-powered group, and small ones, like speaking up at town meetings.

Be prepared to bounce back: Life never goes as we plan. We can't avoid the bumps in the road, and the more risk we take adds more bumps in that road! We all must build those "resilience muscles" to take on the next risk—which might also be the next opportunity.

We control our destinies: We decide the path we want to be on—I, for example, try to be intentional about my direction and drive my path towards a goal. The important thing is that we are making those decisions for ourselves.

In the end, the entire experience of the campaign helped point me in the right direction. I wanted to stay engaged and focused on Connecticut, its problems and solutions.

Over the course of the next few years, I built on what I started in that first campaign. I kept meeting and talking to people around my state. I kept listening, reading and studying. All the while, I noticed that the problems in Connecticut were only getting worse and worse while the rest of the country began to heal from the Great Recession. Even now, Connecticut has only recovered about 78 percent of the jobs lost during the downturn, while every other state has grown its economy beyond prerecession levels.

One night in early 2015, a group of leaders in my community met for dinner in Stamford. The pervasive feeling held by many in the room was that Connecticut had lost its way, that the quality of life and strong economy that once defined the state was fading away and that Hartford politicians were driving the state in the wrong direction. Under Dan Malloy, a second billion-dollar tax increase had just been passed, and more people, including friends, were leaving the state. General Electric, which had moved here back in 1971, had announced that they were starting to look at locations out of state for their business; in talking to GE people, my sense was they felt ignored by officials in Hartford who took them for granted and never called to ask about the company's needs. On top of all that, Connecticut had been ranked one of the worst places to retire in the nation!

At one point during the dinner, one of the business leaders turned to me and said, "Steve, what are you going to do about solving these problems?"

"What am *I* going to do?" I responded. "What are *we* going to do!"

That evening, we planted the seed of "Imagine Connecticut," a civic, community-powered group to discuss the most pressing issues that were destroying our state. The organization would also develop ideas to turn around Connecticut. I stepped up to lead the group under one condition— that it be a solution-oriented action group, not just an outlet to talk shop. Under the "Imagine Connecticut" banner, our single goal was: "Make Connecticut a Top 10 Job Creation State in 10 Years." And why not?

To do this, we created a plan to develop both a fact base to dive deep into the reality of the situation and a strategic plan for Connecticut, just the way I had done for the companies I led. Here were our organizing principles to accomplish this:

- Remember that perfection is not possible;
- Don't get caught in the weeds and lose sight of the goal;
- Figure out where we are and how we got here;
- Define our goals for Connecticut;
- Determine how we measure success;
- Define major strategic options for the state; and
- Believe in an iterative process where people speak their mind, and understand that conflicting opinions drive better outcomes.

We began by studying our past. Connecticut was formed from three settlements of Puritans from Massachusetts and England who came together in 1663 under a single royal charter. Known as "land of steady habits" due to political, social and religious conservatism, Connecticut prospered as an agriculture and trading partner with England. During the American Revolution, the state became a stalwart of the conservative, business-oriented Federalist Party. Connecticut also took a lead in the Industrial Revolution with a strong educational base and an intellectual population led by Yale College and noteworthy people like Mark Twain and Noah Webster. As the demand for work attracted immigrants from Europe, Connecticut developed a great competency in manufacturing, attracted innovators and entrepreneurs and grew a culture of risk-takers. However, the state's economy was overly weighted to military manufacturing through the mid-20th century and exposed itself to federal-government spending cycles, which both helped and hurt over the years. As we know, a shift to lower-cost areas for mass production of industrial and consumer goods has been the dominant trend in the global marketplace. Yet, even with this headwind, Connecticut has maintained a niche, specialty manufacturing market.

As a group, "Imagine Connecticut" believed that with the right policies in place, we could grow from being ranked 48th in business to among the top ten states in which to do business. This is not some far-fetched idea. On economic performance, did you know that Maryland went from 48th to 7th in three years, and North Carolina went from 44th to 13th in four years? By addressing issues like taxes and regulation, workforce quality and cost of living, we believed we could turn around the moving vans and revitalize our state. The core pillars of our vision were built around the development of a strategic plan and solution in five key areas that have proven critical to economic resurgence:

- Job growth and innovation;
- Attraction and retention of people;
- Structure and size of government;
- Quality of life improvement; and
- Investment in our future.

What we found out is that the one thing Connecticut needs to do is install policies that keep people from moving out of state. The exodus from Connecticut is one of the biggest problems to address, and it starts by keeping people here in place. It is really that simple. Jack Mitchell of the famous Westport clothing store, Mitchells, wrote a book entitled "Hug Your Customers." Connecticut needs to hug its "customers"—its citizens and businesses. It needs to listen to them and stop taking advantage of them. For example, making people wait at the Department of Motor Vehicles for hours on end with no other choice is tone-deaf to the challenges of Connecticut's hard-working families. Say you make your living hourly at a fast-food restaurant. How do you get back those four hours of pay? You don't.

We may have lost two Fortune 500 companies in GE and Aetna, but there are still 17 such companies here! Those 17 companies account for thousands of jobs. It is not too late to hug those customers. We have 42 colleges that educate some 250,000 young adults each year, and although 50 percent of them leave the state after they graduate, 50 percent stay. The first step is to make our current customers feel that they are respected, wanted and needed *here*.

That was the thought process around the creation of Imagine Connecticut in 2015. We let the people lead us and tell us what was important to them. We designed a website and launched a Facebook page. We held our own Imagine Connecticut summits and were invited to speak to a number of other groups. In our first year, we had over 15,000 participants join our journey, all wanting to imagine a better, brighter Connecticut.

Again, I realized that I could apply all I had learned in business and the Navy to leading and helping solve problems here at home. Although I could have put my head back down and focused on business or family, I felt there was work to be done to help my state. A single question started to consume me: Connecticut has the same air, earth and water as New York and Massachusetts, so why was Aetna going to New York and GE going to Boston? Then came the moment of realization.

I was driving back from Avon after hosting an Imagine Connecticut summit when I got off I-95 at Exit 27 in Bridgeport. I took a walk around one of those burnt-out manufacturing buildings people drive by all the time. On my walk, I started to ask myself what happened here, and why did it happen? It was then that I realized that, since I graduated from Stamford High School over 30 years before, nothing had changed in Connecticut. In fact, things had gotten only worse: fewer people, fewer jobs, zero economic growth, the loss of GE and Aetna, and all we have to show are rising deficits and taxes, growing debt and this sad statistic—on average, 100 people move out of the state each and every day. Everywhere I go, Connecticut's families, workers and businesses are crying out for bold new leadership with fresh ideas and solutions, not the same old tired policies that protect the status quo in Hartford while the rest of us foot the bill.

The call to serve was clear to me—it was time for our next initiative: Reinvent Connecticut. We can Reinvent Connecticut and our business climate by finally addressing our fiscal mess and making the state a top 10 job creation state once again. We have all the assets and institutions to do just that. We can create a future where Connecticut is once again a center of economic prosperity. We can create a future where people once again feel both physically and financially secure. We can create a future where hard work and opportunities go hand and hand for everyone.

I'll stake my claim and make my stand right here in Connecticut. There is too much to lose if we do nothing, and so much to gain if we forge ahead!

LESSONS LEARNED

- As my friend and mentor, Malcolm Pray, once said, "There are three kinds of people: People who make things happen, people who watch things happen and people who say what happened." You never want to be caught in that last bucket.

- Mobilize people around causes worth fighting for to drive awareness of problems and create real-world solutions.

- Be prepared to bounce back since life never goes as planned. You can't avoid the bumps in the road. You have to build up your "resilience" muscles to take on the next risk and opportunity.

- Aim to serve, not just succeed, by seeking ways to help others with your talents and experiences.

Chapter 13

REINVENTING THE INNOVATION STATE

I am running for Governor to reinvent the culture of Connecticut around vibrant, industry-led ecosystems. I will restore fiscal security to Hartford and financial prosperity for the people of our state.

Leaders—across public office, business, non-profit and academia—must work together to address our fiscal deficit head-on while fostering economic growth where fresh ideas, innovation, rising wages and good jobs are once again our future.

The motto of the State of Connecticut—*"Qui Transtulit Sustinet,"* which translates to "He who transplanted still sustains—has proven not to be the case for the past 30 years. People here have not been able to sustain the quality of life they want for themselves and their families. For those of us in Connecticut, the problems are clear and the results are obvious. The cost of living keeps rising, as do state income taxes and property taxes. Good opportunities are harder to find, many fear the education system won't train them for a good job and houses are staying on the market ever longer at lower prices. Meanwhile, on average 100 people move out of Connecticut each and every day, while an average of around 110 people a day move to Nashville, Tennessee. I believe this is happening because in the 30 years since I graduated from Stamford High School, we have been led by career politicians in

Hartford who care more about preserving the status quo than about giving the citizens and taxpayers of Connecticut a reason to stay. For these 30 years, Connecticut has gone down the path of the politician and it has been a road to ruin. Enough is enough!

I'm not a career politician, my background and experiences are distinctly different from a career politician's, and my path forward will be different for Connecticut. As a naval officer and a high-tech CEO, my path has taken me all over the country and the world. As a result, I understand what motivates people to invest and create jobs and to defend the freedoms we have in this country. I also know what drives people to achieve great opportunities and ensure security for themselves and their families. To that end, I will lay out in this chapter my five-step plan to Reinvent Connecticut. Accomplishing this will require three key elements:

- A visionary leader who sees how Connecticut can once again be the innovation state that we have been before.
- Addressing Connecticut's structural deficits and debt head-on to bring balance back to the state's finances.
- A bold, defined plan that leverages all of Connecticut's assets and focuses our combined interests on expanding opportunity for everyone.

But first, let's talk about the big idea of planting an acorn that can grow into a Charter Oak—a good metaphor when talking about the creation of good jobs in Connecticut. While Aetna and General Electric decided to move out of Connecticut, politicians in Hartford continued to concentrate on the symptom (companies leaving) rather than treating the disease (lack of growth and the current tax and economic policy) that plagues our entire state.

Lost in this current state of crisis management is the root of GE's move and the antidote to the job-destruction cancer afflicting Connecticut. Jeff Immelt, the former chairman and CEO of GE, identified its cause in addressing the Business Council of Fairfield not long ago. "We're a company that doesn't look for special deals," he said, "but we need an ecosystem that's forward-looking, that's future-looking, and that's willing to fight hard to be competitive and enduring for the future." Mark Bertolini, Aetna's Chairman and CEO, said as much in noting that New York provides "the ecosystem of having people in the knowledge economy, working in a town they want to be living in, and we want to attract those folks, and we want to have them on our team."

Ecosystems are important for companies of all sizes, but even more so for a state like Connecticut where almost 80 percent of the people work in small and medium-sized businesses that must innovate in order to survive in a competitive world. In return, this fuels investment in education, the arts, charities and the environment. Once upon a time, Connecticut had a strong ecosystem. Until 1950, 80 percent of Connecticut's economy revolved around designing and building military equipment, and all aspects of Connecticut benefited back then. Things change, however, and if you don't stay on top of key global forces, then people, states and even countries can be left behind. These are the key drivers of why and where ecosystems shift, and we must be aware of them as a state if we want to be a vibrant ecosystem once again:

Opportunity migration: People follow ideas and opportunity, not states! For example, California may be more tax-burdened than Connecticut, yet people tolerate high costs of living for the opportunity to work for a cool company or to realize higher-wage growth.

More world talent: Connecticut used to have a corner on talent. However, there are many more trained, qualified people across the world competing for jobs than there were 50 years ago. We must be competitive in educating and bringing talent together compared to other states and nations.

Impact of automation: Robots, 3D printing and machine learning are automating human jobs. Many of us don't like this reality, but it has been a reality since Johannes Gutenberg created the printing press. We must adapt to this reality and realize that education of our workforce is key to creating new opportunities and industries for our people.

Effect of remote work: The Internet allows people to work anywhere. This allows for remote product and service delivery, like doctors located in the Midwest treating you via your mobile device. That being said, we have to utilize our location as a comparative advantage to other locations.

Having worked in Silicon Valley and seen great economies around the world, I know there are many parts of a successful ecosystem. In my opinion, the key ingredients that need to work together are:

Vibrant Markets: An interconnected network of business, suppliers, customers and government working and competing together.

People: A diverse and broad talent pool to support markets along with academic institutions that boost education and retraining.

Policy: Elected officials who actively engage and understand the implications of inconsistent tax and regulatory policy and uncertainty for long-term decisions that impact not only businesses, but towns, unions and families.

Supports: Transportation and other key infrastructure and support professions that keep systems running on time.

Finance: Money to support the range of activity from infrastructure to business needs.

Culture: A creative and risk-taking attitude that generates world-changing products and services.

As a CEO, I know how to mobilize these resources and elements to Connecticut's advantage. Politicians who have never experienced this have no idea about the interplay between these forces. Ecosystems, like Silicon Valley's technology area or London as a financial capital, take time and hard work to create, but historically they have benefited from a galvanizing call to action with transformative goals. Think about Kennedy's moonshot, Google's driverless car and Bill Gates' "Malaria No More" initiatives. Mayor Michael Bloomberg realized that New York City had to adjust to shifting economic forces. After much planning, the Roosevelt Island Cornell Tech project was hatched to lay the groundwork for economic expansion beyond retail and financial services. Opened in 2017 with over two million square feet of space, Roosevelt Island will bring together academics, entrepreneurs, investors and multinational companies to expand New York's future prospects.

Connecticut has all the assets to mount a successful turnaround. The first is location—one of our chief advantages. We are an hour and a half from New York City and Boston. One-third of the entire U.S. economy lies within 500 miles of Connecticut, and 40 million consumers live within a 200-mile radius of our state. We live along the I-95, I-91 and I-84 corridors, with access to major airports and seaports across the state. We have a vibrant arts and museum community. Our 42 institutions of higher education annually educate more than 250,000 students with the potential to fill high-paying jobs in finances, technology and industry. Yet half of these kids upon graduation have to leave Connecticut to find good-paying jobs. This has to change.

Now is the time for Connecticut to embark on our own journey to rebuild vibrant ecosystems around world-class, applied-research universities and core industries dedicated to our state, where we compete successfully compared to other states. Some of these academic institutions are here already, but we could attract others to our great state, thereby attracting local and global businesses as well. We actually have at least three core industries to build upon where we are among the best in the world. Finance and insurance is a strong competency of our state, and it still represents one of the largest parts of our economy. Life sciences and healthcare delivery are industries where we have innovated and have world-class institutions. Finally, we have the world's largest helicopter, jet-engine and submarine maker here. The trend toward advanced manufacturing is key and can allow us to compete once again. We just need to be more rigorous and disciplined in how we manage our state finances so that these institutions feel as if they are partners on a worthwhile journey, rather than simply a bottomless ATM for the state.

Once this is done, we can locate these applied-research universities and corporations in and around our major cities while we recast our urban centers for future growth. Our cities have remained small and subscale for too long; we should be utilizing them and the suburbs to create growth engines again. Then, we will be able to overlap our transportation efforts to speed our trains, embrace autonomous driving and rethink our roads to link these cities into larger-scale population centers. Think of it this way: if we can move people among New Haven, Bridgeport and Stamford, within, say, 30 minutes, we'll have created the third-largest population center in the Northeast after New York and

Boston. We would be larger and have a better geographic location than Providence, Springfield and Albany to attract jobs. Linking in Hartford to this expanded network and leveraging its position between New York and Boston would only strengthen the value proposition. That will drive people and jobs back to Connecticut.

A return to a strong, forward-looking, industry-led ecosystem is the transformative seed we must plant to create a garden of opportunity that will close Connecticut's expanding gaps in skills, income and education. This stance will also help address our state's fiscal challenges. Reinventing Connecticut is the way forward. To create and execute this new vision, we must evaluate a leader's abilities on three dimensions: experience and values, quality of ideas and ability to execute ideas. The absence of any one aspect will lead to failure, but maximizing all three will enable Connecticut to thrive once again.

Steve Jobs once said, "He who can't change his ideas is a prisoner of his past." Connecticut needs to change her ideas because the ideas of leaders for the past 30 years haven't served the state or her citizens well. This next election needs to be about bold, fresh, innovative ideas that will reinvigorate Connecticut and reverse the downward spiral she's on.

Ideas must be communicated by leaders. The captain of my submarine taught me a very valuable lesson in leadership when he said: "Leaders set tone, tone creates a culture, and culture is destiny." Career politicians in Hartford drone on about a "new economic reality" of fixed costs and that "manufacturing is never coming back." We don't need this negativity and hand-wringing. We need a chief executive who has achieved success in the toughest of times, someone who has ideas and a plan and is enthusiastic about Connecticut's potential.

As my background, experiences and path are different than those of the career politicians in Hartford, so too will my tone be different and, with it, my plan for the future of our state.

Connecticut hasn't been a job-creation engine in a long time, but we can change that. It starts with a vision, which will create a culture of innovators, which will lead to a better future. A culture of innovators was our past, and it can be our future. This process won't be easy, and it won't happen overnight. However, great achievements have always started with a clear vision to get up every Monday morning and get to work. Let me share with you my five-step plan to Reinvent Connecticut:

Step 1: Make State Government Smaller and More Efficient
The role of government is to deliver quality services to citizens at the best cost possible. For years, the opposite has been the culture of Connecticut state government—ask anyone who has endured a four-hour CT Department of Motor Vehicle wait. Discipline in government spending is key to our turnaround. It is time to balance the budget without gimmicks, tax increases, temporary monies, and borrowed funds. We must implement outcome-based budgeting instead of simply increasing spending year after year. In business, we use benchmark and best- practice strategies. This means that we must compare ourselves to other states, and we need to get our overspending in line.

In addition, we need to apply commonsense business practices to reduce the cost of government and improve customer service. As a CEO, I have done this for federal and state governments as well as businesses. Regarding our state pension plans, it is time to bring fiscal security to all state employees and teachers in an affordable framework.

We need to explore aligning state-employee pension contributions with other states to provide stability to these plans. The outcome of Step 1 will enable us to right-side our spending and deliver a sustainable and high-quality customer experience to the taxpayers of Connecticut.

Step 2: Make Connecticut More Affordable

Each day, droves of Connecticut residents leave the state as the cost of living continues to drive people away. Turning the moving vans around must start with reducing the tax burden that many people feel has come to define Connecticut over the past 30 years. It is time to vigorously reduce taxes. From 2012 to 2015, Connecticut lost $6.2 billion of adjusted gross income—or four percent of total government receipts. Beyond protecting and helping people who can't take care of themselves, government's aim should be for its citizens to keep as much of their paycheck in their pockets so they can choose what to do with it. This will enable more money being put into our economy instead of our government. Consumer and business spending grow an economy, but government spending does not. Let the people decide where to spend their hard-earned money—whether it be on charities, retirement, building a business, buying a home or simply saving for a rainy day.

We must look to systematically reduce the taxes to make Connecticut more affordable. This can be accomplished in two phases. First, let's immediately enact a tax policy to retain people committed to Connecticut regardless of whether they are seniors in retirement, hard-working folks or young families just getting started. We can bring tax relief immediately to our citizens. Second, the benefits of Step 1—Make State Government Smaller and More Efficient—will allow broad-based tax reductions to provide everyone relief from the overspending in Hartford. This will reduce the cost of living in Connecticut. Simply said, lowering state taxes will retain people in our state to grow our economy.

Step 3: Make it Easier to Start a Business and Live Here

Connecticut needs to be simplified. Currently, it is too complicated and expensive to do business here. For starters, we must make it easier to start a business by imposing a regulatory freeze and beginning a comprehensive review of current and pending regulations that work against this objective. We must pursue regulatory reform to expedite permits, especially for job-creating industries. We need to look at creating a "SEAL team" of business advisers that will work to get people into business as opposed to scaring people away from it; it should be their job to get people through the red tape, not wrap them up in it. The same applies to looking rigorously at unfunded mandates that do more to slow progress than anything else. Our regulations must look to make us more competitive with other states across several categories, such as transportation, healthcare and energy costs.

Step 4: Retain Jobs and Grow the Economy

As Governor, I will fight tirelessly every day to work with current and potential businesses to grow our economy. We need to exploit the Internet and local economic development offices that will be critical to retaining and growing businesses. The centralized Hartford model doesn't work. These local offices will have the right level of resources, and our SEAL team of experts will help businesses navigate the state and local regulatory process in a fast, lowest-cost manner, as well as providing help on state and federal grants.

To do this, we must eliminate overlapping efforts in Hartford and have one group that works with local economic-development offices. I will do away with the "First Five" program of millions of dollars of corporate giveaways. Instead, I will streamline the more than 27 tax credits, looking to replace them with one simple idea. Here is what I am looking at: If you are a business—small, medium or large—and are committed to hiring people in our state, you will get an annual tax credit associated with that employee hire for, say, five years. Whether you are a Fortune 500 company or a small business owner, we need and must reward those who hire full-time workers and create jobs for our neighbors.

Step 5: Create Industry Ecosystems That Attract and Retain Talent

We need to keep our people and talent local. With ecosystem models like Roosevelt Island in mind, I will work to attract and retain businesses and talent to create industry-cluster ecosystems around applied research, university tech transfer, laboratories and business incubators. This will require public-private partnerships and joint investment with world-class universities and businesses to create technology clusters around our natural areas of strength. These unique clusters include the key industries of healthcare, finance and insurance and advanced manufacturing.

We must drive the impact of in-state university research and connect it to the economic development efforts at the local and national levels. This will allow us to strengthen and invest in our cities and surrounding suburbs. Our cities are our future, and we must work to bring them back from ruin and bankruptcy with a sustainable economic model grounded in technology and business investment.

Within these industry ecosystems, we can also apply a similar model to community colleges and the trades professions. This is also needed to address the shortfall of talent for many important jobs—for example, training people to care for our seniors and kids as well as rebuilding our state, buildings, highways and homes. One thing I am looking at is how we can use retired professionals to give back by having them train the next generation to transform and lead Connecticut. We can work smarter on bringing innovative solutions, but it will take planning, execution and grit. Underlying this initiative is preserving and improving our pre-K to 12 education system that is under increasing pressure. We need to address head on the funding and standards issues in particular and how we use technology and innovation to ensure our children get the skills they need to thrive in the 21st century.

Finally, we must look at using and creating innovative transportation networks to link our communities and overcome the small size of our state. However, the ability to move jobs to people and people to jobs quickly will overcome this shortcoming and allow us to draw people once again to Connecticut as opposed to simply becoming a "drive-through" state.

As stated at the outset of the chapter, I am running for Governor to Reinvent Connecticut. My plan will restore fiscal security to our state as we address our growing deficits and enable vibrant, industry-led ecosystems that allow small, medium and large businesses to thrive again. This will re-ignite a culture of innovation and possibilities and will rebuild our urban cores necessary for our long-term growth and competitiveness. I want to enable a state where all of us have the ability and opportunities to pursue our ambitions and dreams.

Doing this won't be easy, of course. The things worth fighting for in life rarely are. Let me end with a challenge. For 30 years, we've been heading down a path created by career politicians. It has proven to be a road to ruin. As the poet Robert Frost predicted in his famous poem "The Road Not Taken," we are finally at that fork in the road. And as Yogi Berra quipped, "When you come to the fork in the road, take it!" Well, the other fork leads to my path—the path of the Stamford kid, military veteran and job builder. So, do you want to stay on the path of the politician, or go down a new path of the job creator and innovator? Job creation and innovation have been our history, and I believe it can be our future once again.

I look forward to writing the next chapter of our state's history with the people of Connecticut. The career politicians in Hartford have had their chance. Now it's our turn. It's time to Reinvent Connecticut—together.

LEADERSHIP LESSONS

- Steve Jobs once said, "He who can't change his ideas is a prisoner of his past." Connecticut must have different leadership because the ideas of its leaders for the past 30 years have taken us down a road to ruin.

- Leaders must bring tested experience, innovative ideas and the ability to execute in order to enact real, enduring change.

- Reinventing Connecticut will take restoring fiscal security and building vibrant, industry-led ecosystems to retain and attract businesses and people to our state.

LESSONS LEARNED

CHAPTER 1:
RUNNING SILENT, RUNNING DEEP

- Run toward the fire: Simply said, confront the crisis, don't shrink from it. You'll never gain control if you run away from the crisis.

- Prepare for the mission moment: There are few times in our lives when all the training and preparation that you do lead to a finite moment of importance. That moment on the battlefield, in business or in a personal challenge is the culmination of planning, execution and grit.

CHAPTER 2:
THE FOUNDATIONS OF LEADERSHIP

- Choose a path for your family: The courage to make decisions that are right for a person and a family set in place unknown benefits and yield opportunities for generations to follow.

- Defer gratification: I learned from my grandparents to work hard, be a good person, trust in myself and strive to keep dessert where it is meant to be—at the end of the meal, not at the beginning.

CHAPTER 3:
ROLE MODELS AT HOME

- Challenging yet supportive environments allow people to develop at their own rate to achieve their potential.

- Open yourself to watching and listening to others around you: Everyone has something to teach you.

- Ronald Reagan once said, "The family has always been the cornerstone of American society. Our families nurture, preserve and pass on to each succeeding generation the values we share and cherish."

CHAPTER 4:
STAMFORD, THE CITY THAT WORKED FOR A KID

- Let your childhood open your eyes to the world around you to imagine new possibilities.

- Cities can expand a child's view of the world and are vital to a state's social, economic and cultural health.

- Seek diversity to understand different perspectives and develop solutions that aren't one-dimensional.

CHAPTER 5:
ANNAPOLIS: LEARNING TO LEAD

- Learn to follow: In order to be a leader, you must first learn how to follow others.

- Focus on the needs and desires of people: The perspective and empathy that comes from this allows you to better align a team's or institution's common interests.

- Discipline involves learning to do the right thing when no one is watching.

- Dedicate yourself to a project or cause bigger than yourself.

CHAPTER 6:
FORGING CHARACTER UNDER THE POLAR ICE CAP

- Treat others with respect, regardless of their standing in the crew or community.

- Don't be a "sea lawyer," who makes excuses for his actions: Own up to your actions and take responsibility.

- Set a tone of what is possible: Tone creates culture and culture is destiny.

- Train your instincts to be ready to make decisions: If you need 100 percent confidence before making them, you'll probably miss the opportunities you are after.

CHAPTER 7:
WHARTON: TRANSITIONING FROM THE MILITARY TO THE BUSINESS WORLD

- Transitions have their own timetables and agendas. They come at the cost of leaving where we are and what we know, and they're usually necessitated by a deep desire to grow and to thrive.

- Realize and value the power of mentors, friends and relationships. First and foremost, they make up the very fabric of a life well lived.

- World-class athletes often talk about being on a "fast field" that makes them play at their best. We all get better when we are around people who push us to attain our goals.

CHAPTER 8:
LEARNING TO INNOVATE

- Begin with what is impossible and make it possible.

- Don't try to force a plant from a seed. Ideas take time. You have to commit to the idea and dance with it as it changes and grows.

- There are no golden rules in entrepreneurship, no perfect idea or opportunity, and no perfect time to start. You just have to start going down the path.

- De-myth the idea of the individual hero: Entrepreneurship and business are team sports, and strong teams are more about the chemistry of the people as a whole than about the biology of any one person.

CHAPTER 9:
GROWING A TECHNICAL BUSINESS IN A COMPLEX WORLD

- Business is about people and relationships. These interactions strengthen when people are able to come together and spend time together solving problems.

- Understand and embrace the advances in technology at the risk of getting left behind. We must improve educational outcomes to ensure opportunity for everyone.

- Nurture talent by investing in the people around you to strengthen an organization. None of us is permanent in any role and we have to leave an institution stronger than how we found it.

CHAPTER 10:
COMING BACK HOME TO CONNECTICUT

- Home should not just be where our families are but where we find the opportunities to pursue our passions and careers while positively impacting our communities.

- To make a state or region viable to attract people today requires applied-research universities that create new ideas and solutions working in concert with businesses, small and large, to get new ideas to market to change people's lives.

- There are no enduring overnight-success stories in business. Building companies and creating real jobs take time and a whole lot of hard work.

CHAPTER 11:
CREATING JOBS FOR THE FUTURE

- Trust is the intangible force that increases the speed of forming relationships and results.

- Complement your blind spots: Truly value the different skills and DNA of others.

- Be ready to confront and overcome the three phases of commercial acceptance: ridicule, opposition and self-evidence.

- Create a sense of destination and destiny in your team.

CHAPTER 12:
A CALL TO SERVE AGAIN

- As my friend and mentor, Malcolm Pray, once said, "There are three kinds of people: People who make things happen, people who watch things happen and people who say what happened." You never want to be caught in that last bucket.

- Mobilize people around causes worth fighting for to drive awareness of problems and create real-world solutions.

- Be prepared to bounce back since life never goes as planned. You can't avoid the bumps in the road. You have to build up your "resilience" muscles to take on the next risk and opportunity.

- Aim to serve, not just succeed, by seeking ways to help others with your talents and experiences.

CHAPTER 13:
REINVENTING THE INNOVATION STATE

- Steve Jobs once said, "He who can't change his ideas is a prisoner of his past." Connecticut must have different leadership because the ideas of its leaders for the past 30 years have taken us down a road to ruin.

- Leaders must bring tested experience, innovative ideas and the ability to execute in order to enact real, enduring change.

- Reinventing Connecticut will take restoring fiscal security and building vibrant, industry-led ecosystems to retain and attract businesses and people to our state.